EATING BITTERNESS:

A VISION BEYOND THE PRISON WALLS

Front Cover: THE STRENGTH AND THE ANGER

This painting is a tribute to my aunt and uncle Eva and Art Solomon.

The eagle that surrounds Eva represents the gift of strength that she shares to keep both her and Art walking that difficult path they travel. It has been her unwavering faith and strength that enables Art to continue his work.

The bear that surrounds Art represents the anger that he feels when dealing with a foreign establishment that has brought so much misery to our people. The bear also symbolizes the healing that is struggling to surface within the walls of the prisons.

The four stars that sparkle in the sky are the four directions in the world that these two helpers have travelled.

In the far-off distance are the two worlds that exist: the natural world of the mountains, and unnatural, artificial structures of the city. In the middle of the clash between these two are the lost souls of our people that dominate the populations in the prisons, yet are so alone. The eagle is screaming for "Life" and the skull is the ever-present element of "Death".

At the bottom is the strength of the Eagle Feather that has brought Eva and Art to this place on their paths and can give life meaning to our brothers and sisters who so desperately need it.

Perry McLeod-Shabogesic

EATING BITTERNESS:

A VISION BEYOND THE PRISON WALLS

Poems and Essays of

ART SOLOMON

Edited by

Cathleen Kneen and Michael Posluns

NC Press Limited

Toronto, 1994

Cover painting and interior drawings by Perry McLeod-Shabogesic
Back cover photograph of Art Solomon copyright Toronto Star Syndicate,
used by permission
Cover design by Nash & Nash Ltd.
Interior design by Cathleen Kneen

Canadian Cataloguing in Publication Data

Main Entry under title:
Solomon, Arthur
    Eating bitterness : visions beyond the prison wall
ISBN 1-55021-084-X
1. Indians of North America – Religion and
mythology – Poetry. 2. Indians of North America –
Pastoral counseling of. 3. Religious work with
prisoners. I. Title.
PS8587.04195E43 1994   299'.7   C94-932777-8
PR9199.3.S65E43 1994

We would like to thank the Ontario Arts Council, the Ontario Publishing
Centre, the Ontario Ministry of Culture, Tourism and Recreation, the
Ontario Development Corporation, the Canada Council and the Government
of Canada, Department of Canadian Heritage and the Association for the
Export of Canadian Books for their assistance in the production and marketing of
this book.

New Canada Publications, a division of NC Press Limited,
Box 452, Station A, Toronto, Ontario, Canada, M5W 1H8.

Printed and bound in Canada

ACKNOWLEDGEMENTS

I want to thank the many people whose care in preserving my writings over the years has made this book possible. In particular, I must mention Menno Wiebe, Dr. Ed Newbery and his wife Rena. Rarihokwats and Joan Kuyek also helped. Special thanks to Phyllis Fischer, who worked hard to make the vision a reality.

Perry McLeod-Shabogesic's painting for the cover and other artwork is a gift to be treasured.

I also want to thank Michael Posluns and Cathleen Kneen, without whose dedication and persistence this book would not have been made.

Finally, of course, I must honour and give thanks to my wife Eva, who continues to be the strength and support of all my work.

I first met Art Solomon in 1962, when the fog was just lifting enough that he could see the Good Red Road which he would follow for the rest of his life. In that journey, he has never wavered, never compromised, never rested, never looked back. He knew what was the right thing, and he did it.

Art's decision was worse than unpopular. He was misunderstood, resented, criticized, scrutinized, harassed and rejected. "Of course you are right," he would be told, "but . . ." and then would come the stream of excuses and rationalizations about "being practical", "being reasonable", "you can't go back".

It would have been easier, of course, if Art Solomon had been born Kesheyanakwan, instead of having to become him. His life has been an unfinished work in progress, and Art has been its principal craftsman, sculpting the Creator's original material with the guidance of Spirit Winds. All the original ingredients are still visible, but his life's shape today could not have been seen, even imagined, until he was well into middle-age years. He evolved into someone else right before the disbelieving eyes of family and friends who were not yet prepared to join Art on the path he was taking.

The events of the 1970s brought Native Peoples into the nation's living-rooms. Native crafts went into fancy galleries. Instant "medicine men" appeared on talk-shows. Buckskin and beads became high fashion. Art Solomon was well-positioned to gain prestige, praise, and prominence, but he never varied either pace or direction. He continued to utter unspeakable truths in blunt terms. He scorned urban comforts, preferring to be in the bush with Creation's riches or in the prisons with Creation's forgotten people.

We journeyed together with White Roots of Peace/Four Arrows. He was a powerful teacher, an avid student, a joyful traveller. Eva was always there, always cheerful. Art was the light, Eva the fuel. His gifts to me that I treasure most were a homemade axe-handle and a hand-carved yoke for carrying buckets of water.

Just by being himself, however, Art created more than his share of enemies. Persons prepared to take only half-measures felt criticized by his mere presence. Government people found him unsusceptible to those rewards offered to Native leaders willing to become cooperative. Many Native people considered Art a threat to their own hard-won "progress". He took the pain of it all in stride. It would have been enough if he just took the blows which unavoidably came his way — but he added to them by insisting on pushing ahead where he knew he must go without regard to the personal sacrifices which he knew would be required.

To many, Art has seemed to be a demanding teacher, unforgiving and uncompromising. Yet he has never asked anyone to follow him. He held out truths rather than expectations. While he would not allow dodging the fact that we all have choices, he had no imperatives. "What I have to say will hurt many ears, but I have to say it," he would say. That was his duty. You could do your own duty as you saw fit, and that was your problem, your opportunity, not his.

Kesheyanakwan had heard the Creator's Instructions, and he understood his responsibility to follow them the best way he possibly could. He applied his free will to take and determine his direction, and he turned to the Creation to sustain his energies. He has found it is so simple to do that he must ponder, I am sure, why everyone else does not do the same.

This book will offer strength and encouragment to all those who wish to take their own journey on the Good Red Road which has been laid out for them.

CONTENTS

THE CRIMINAL "JUST US" SYSTEM

THERE WILL BE JUSTICE

INTRODUCTION

ART SOLOMON'S INTRODUCTION OF HIMSELF

I was born in August 1913, in Killarney, Ontario
on the north shore of Georgian Bay
of a French mother and an Ojibway father.

I was sent to a residential school
at Spanish, Ontario,
where I passed Grade 8.
I was sent back to Killarney without a certificate
and I was put into Grade 6
without an assessment being done.

I was fifteen years old when my dad died.
1928, December the 28th.
After I went to Spanish,
there was no contact until summertime.
Then he was away guiding. He was
a good man. The best guide
in that part of the country.

At age 16, I walked out of school.
I didn't drop out
I walked out.
And I never went back again.

I did take a correspondence course
in aeronautical engineering.
I was fascinated with flying.

In 1933, I started to work as a fisherman.

In Killarney in 1936, I began work
as a pulp cutter, road builder, carpenter,
boatbuilder, blacksmith, farmer, hunter,
logger, anything to survive in the Depression.

In 1937-1944, I worked as a miner in Sudbury,
then as a carpenter for Ontario Hydro.
I'm not aware I had any dreams.
I was struggling so hard,
just to keep body and soul together for myself
and for my family.

In the early 1950s, I was asked to join
the Nickel Belt Indian Club. That's when
I decided to identify myself as a Native person
I knew it was the hard way to go.

I had been Catholic. Somewhere,
I came to the conclusion
that the Church had lost its message.
They could talk about it,
but they couldn't live it.
I got interested in the Midewiwin Society.

I became a Born-Again Pagan.

I realized I was changing the world
because I was changing me,
and that's where you begin.
That's the important place.

For a long time I was alone.
But I never got discouraged.

In 1964, I was a founding member
of the World Crafts Council founded
at Columbia University, New York City.

In 1965 January, I was a founding member
at Winnipeg, Manitoba
of the Canadian Craftsmens' Association
and I was a councillor-at-large for some years.

In 1968, I put together what was called
Indian Crafts of Ontario with a grant
of two hundred thousand dollars
from the Ontario government.
I paid for the incorporation out of my own pocket
and hand-picked the first Board of Directors
from prominent Native and non-Native people of Ontario.

I have lectured at many universities in North America
in the past 20 years and in Europe as well.

I am a founding member
of the Native Studies Department of the University of Sudbury
and as a result of my work in prisons,
we devised a curriculum for Native people in prison
which has been, and still is, being taught
in the prisons of Ontario.

I am also a member of the Spiritual Elders Council
for the Kingston Area Federal Prisons.

At the 6th Assembly of the World Council of Churches
in Vancouver in July-August 1983,
I was one of the 15 guests of W.C.C., the only Native person
to be invited from the world community.

I have been an active member of the World Conference
on Religion and Peace,
and I was a member of a small committee
involved with the planning for a consultation
by the World Council of Churches
with 15 Native spiritual leaders in Canada in 1987.

I was in Holland on a speaking tour and
someone described me as a medicine man.
I discourage that. I don't claim anything for
myself except to be another human being.
I'm in the business of helping people

to help themselves, to see things differently
to understand that there are choices to be made.

I used to judge other people.
I was given the revelation that I didn't have
the ability to judge anyone
not even myself.
All I can say is that gradually,
I have been taught by the Creator.

These are some of the things
that I have been
and that I am presently involved with.

*(Persons wishing to know more about Art Solomon's life
will find extensive biographical information
in his first book, Songs of the People.)*

THE FIVE-YEAR PLAN

I was told by the doctor in Sudbury
I was finished.

So I moved back to Killarney,
and the family stayed in West Bay for a while.

And what I did was I made myself
a 5-year plan, because I figured
that maybe I wasn't going to make it
because I had a deadly disease called
Bright's Disease. I took some years
to try and find out what the hell it meant.

Being very unfit to work,
I couldn't take a job no place anywheres.
Some days I couldn't work at all.
So I made a garden, for one thing.
I put my head down and ploughed.

So the first five years went by
and I was still alive.

And so I made another five-year plan.

HOW DOES AN ELDER BECOME AN ELDER?

Somebody asked that question a couple of years ago
written in a note by
a woman with the mind of a mouse.
She never had accepted her responsibility
for who she was and why she was here
in this part of Creation.

She asked me the question
because she would have liked to have been there.

I said the elders are chosen by the people
who know the leaders who have been
chosen by God.

I had the experience some years ago
of asking God if I could help
with Her Work, with His Work.

And gradually over time I realized
I was already helping the Creator
with Her Work because I was helping
the People
and that's the only way
it can be done.

HONOURS AWARDED TO ART SOLOMON:

Citizenship of the Year Award, Sudbury, 1984
LL.D. Laurentian University, 1986
D.D. Queen's University, 1988
Medal of Merit from the Government of Ontario, 1989
LL.D. Concordia University, 1992

NOT DISAPPEARING

We the Native people of Canada
    have the highest rate of suicide in this country.
It is said to be four times the national average.
Last summer there were nine young people who committed suicide
    at Povungnituk, a village on the east coast of Hudson Bay.
And two nights ago we heard on national television
    that a community of people wanted to move
    from where they were at Davis Inlet
    an island on the Labrador coast
    to somewhere else, because of the desperate
    circumstances that the people were in and
    because of the high rate of suicide of their young people.
The people had been moved to a desolate land from where
    they had lived in northern Quebec for years.
They were Innu people who had been promised
    by the government of KKKanada
    that they would find better hunting
    and a better life in that far away land.
What they found was a disaster instead.
And a government who couldn't care less
    about what happened to the people.
Obviously the government of KKKanada had other plans
    which they never told the people about.
It was a disaster from the start and still is.
Which is proof again — if any proof is needed —
    that we, the aboriginal people of this land,
    cannot trust our lives or our well-being
    to the promises and the cold clammy hands
    of the governments of this country.

Since they came to this sacred land five hundred years ago
    they have done everything in their power
    to make us disappear.

They have used guns and treachery.
They have used diseased blankets.
They have used laws and lies.
They have used prisons
    and starvation.
They have used policies of assimilation
    and deliberate genocide.
They have used policies of sterilization
    against our women.
They said they were Christian and civilized.
They said we were savages and pagans
    and that we worshipped evil spirits.
That is how their history books are written
    and that is still how it is today.
They have despised and hated us.
They have tried everything in their power to make us go away.
But we are still here.
And we will still be here when they are gone.

They came to this sacred land five hundred years ago.
It was a paradise when they came
    and they turned it into a living hell for us
    the original people who were put here on this land
    by the Creator God.
We did not cross the Bering Strait
    as the anthropologists insist.
We are not the lost tribe of Israel.
We were put on this land by the Creator God
    to take care of it for those who would come after us;
    to leave a clean and beautiful place for them to walk on.
A land of peace and plenty where future generations
    could live out and accomplish their destiny
    as they were intended by the Creator God.
We could not own what belongs only
    to the One who created it.

The strangers who came to this sacred land
        came with a philosophy based
        on a *false concept of ownership*.
They could own anything they could get their hands on,
        including a vast grant of land that was given
        to the honourable company of gentlemen
        trading into Hudson's Bay.
They could raise armies
        but they could not fight against Christian princes;
        everyone else was fair game.

The treaties that they made with the people who lived here –
I have called them *Documents of Deceit*,
        because of the more than four hundred treaties
        that were signed in the United States of Amerikkka,
        they never kept but one: they promised to take
        the land and they took it.
Last summer in a court case in British Columbia
        that lasted for two years and cost the people of the
        Gitksan Wetsu'weten nations millions of dollars,
        the judge said that the people who had lived
        on the land for a hundred thousand years
        did not own the land that they lived on:
        they had no right to live there;
        the land belonged to the government of British Columbia
        and the people could be dispossessed
        at the pleasure of the government at any time.

That is the kind of justice we have been exposed to
        in this land for five hundred years.
All that we are asking from the people of this land
        is Justice.
We are not going to ask from
        the *Criminal "Just Us" System,* and
        we are not going to ask from
        the criminal, captive, state governments of this country
        because they do not understand what it means.

The people who lived in this land for
     a hundred thousand years
     lived by a philosophy based on
     the power and the beauty
     the sacredness and the harmony
     of the Creation. We were the caretakers of this land;
     not the owners, because we could not own
     what belongs to God.
We understood that as children of the Creator God
we are all less than perfect.
Our work here in this part of Creation
     was to work as best we could toward our perfection,
     so that when we have to go back to the spirit world
     where we came from,
     we will be able to answer the question:
     "What have you done with the time
     and the opportunities and the gifts
     that I gave to you?"

TEACHINGS

THE SEVEN FIRES

In times gone by, the Ojibway religious teachings tell us, seven major prophets came to the Anishnabe. Each prophet left with his people a prediction about what the future would bring. Each of these prophesies was called a fire. Each of these fires referred to a particular period or era of time. Thus, the teachings of the seven prophets are called the seven fires.

The first fire tells us that the Ojibway nation would rise
    and follow the sacred shell.
      The religion would serve as a rallying point for the Anishnabe
      and the traditional ways of the Midewiwin religion would
      be the source of much strength.

The second fire tells that the nation would be camped
    by a large body of water.
      In this time, the direction of the sacred shell would be
      lost, and the religion would be weak.
      It was said that a boy would be born to point the way
      back to the traditional ways.
      He showed the direction to the stepping stones of
      the Manitoulin Island chain,
      here much rebirth of religious beliefs occurred.

The third fire tells that the Ojibway people would find
    the path to their chosen ground . . .
    a land in the west to which they must move their families.

The fourth fire tells of the coming of the light-skinned race.

The fifth fire relates to us a great struggle that was to come.

The sixth fire tells us that during this time grandsons and
    granddaughters would turn against their elders and the
    spiritual ways of the Ojibway would almost disappear.

The seventh fire tells of the emergence of a new people,
    a people that would retrace their steps to find the
    sacred ways that had been left behind,
    the waterdrum would once again sound its voice,
    there would be a re-birth of the Ojibway nation
    and a re-kindling of old fires.
    At this time the light-skinned race would be given a choice,
    if they would chose the right road,
    then the seventh fire would light the eighth and final —
    fire — an eternal fire of peace, love, and brotherhood.
    If the light-skinned race would make the wrong
    choice of roads
    then the destruction which they brought with them
    on coming to this great island,
    would come back to them and cause much
    death and suffering.
    That is the story of the seven fires.

January, 1976

ANISHNABEG
Children of the Seventh Fire

Theresa Solomon-Gravel
12 July 1994

That's us.
How many generations are there
Within 100 years?

It has been over that
Since They have been among Us
In this land they call "Canada"

In their effort to "help"
They have nearly destroyed us
Our Elders and Our Ancestors

But we are Children of the Seventh Fire
Our destiny has already been written
In the words of the Prophets
Of our Ancestors

It's up to us now
To take our turn
To do our part

And so
Children of the Seventh Fire
Take those words
And give them life
Learn them
Know them
Share them
Hold fast to them
And teach them
To your children
For it is within them

That you will find
The strength and the wisdom of the Elders
Our Ancestors

The Knowledge
The Key
It's there
In the words of the Prophets of the Seventh Fire

Travel back
Along the trail
And pick up the bundles
The knowledge that is there,
Learn it
Protect it
Care for it
Share it
For we are Children of the Seventh Fire

It is our turn now
To make the prophecies come true
The Gift of this Knowledge
Is the answer to our furture

For we are Children of the Seventh Fire

A LETTER TO J.B. CUSTER
at Pelican Narrows, August 5, 1991

Dear John,

I have kept your letter of April 19, 1991 till now. I have been travelling some since then. I will be part of a traditional wedding here on August 9, and I will be going up to Amos, Quebec on August 14 for a meeting and teaching with the Algonquin youth council of Northern Quebec until August 19 or 20. Then back home for a short while.

I would like to think that perhaps we could begin correspondence for a while. Obviously your community is in trouble and searching for direction. There is a direction for us to go as Native people after the devastation of Christianity and civilization. we have to make a choice now. The choice for me is very clear. The imperative for us as Aboriginal people is to heal ourselves, heal our communities, and heal our nations. In doing that we will be healing the earth mother as well.

The healing power that we will use is L-O-V-E — it is profoundly simple but that doesn't mean that it is easy to do. It means going back to the profoundly simple ways that we once lived. It means rejecting the ways of that violent society that came here five hundred years ago.

> *They came in violence*
> *They have lived in violence*
> *And they will go in violence*
> *But it will not be the violence*
> *Of the aboriginal people of this land*

Because remember what God said in the Bible: *Do not revenge because vengeance is mine alone.* So we leave that part to God which makes it so much more simple for us. It means that we are responsible for our own healing because we are the final teachers in this sacred land.

We cannot help others to heal if we are sick ourselves. And we are sick psychologically, mentally, spiritually. We can and we will heal those of us who are determined for that to happen. We have a free will and we have a total responsibility for that free will. Which means that we have no right to require others to follow the direction that we are going. All that we can do is share with others and let them choose their own way. This may sound a little like pie in the sky but it really isn't. If I have to speak about life, I have to say that *in its vast complexity is its profound simplicity*. That is the reality.

Although we were less than perfect as people are (as long as we live in these human bodies) we lived by the teachings of Christ thousands of years before we heard of them. We had a responsibility to care for everyone in our community from the very youngest to the very oldest and all the way in between — which means that we had the best insurance policy that was ever devised.

So we have to look back to see how it was in order to find our way ahead. It is vastly simpler than we think. We have to do something about our messed up minds. We can see that the man's way doesn't work for us and not even for him. We know we got into the mess that we are in, and just as sure as we know that we also know our way back out. The man doesn't know his way back out.

We are the final teachers in this sacred land to teach others how to live in harmony with the creation; that means also how to live in harmony with men and women and children. To do that means that we have to step back and allow women to take their rightful place in the human family, because they are the real leaders and the best leaders in the human family. We as men have to begin to honour and respect our women again and hear what they are trying to say to us. They also must take the garbage out of their heads and put good things back in.

We have to learn together. We have to heal together. We can do that and we will do that. The process has already begun. What we need more than anything else is strong clear minded women because they are the foundation of our nations; and strong clear minded women automatically make strong clear minded men; so I have to help the women to find their own way again.

I think it would be excellent if you could get this letter typed and return it to me, because I need to write a lot more to go with this; and also to share it with other people where you live. That way we might be able to accomplish some "long distance healing" as it were.

I'm going to send a copy of a paper by Jeanette Armstrong. I have her permission to share it with others. It would be good if you could share it with other women and men. I'm serious about corresponding with you. I hope that you can send me a typed copy back. Who knows, it might become a book to help others.

With love from Art Solomon

POEMS FOR SPECIAL PEOPLE (1):
To Ed Glover

A Father, Husband, and Grandfather,
It's hard to find the words to say
To a brother, and a friend of many years
Yet somehow they must be said today.

As I look out on this world that I live in
I see that trouble and hurt abound,
But through all the years I've known you
I've known a happy man
A man who always knew how to celebrate life
No matter how hard the way ahead.

I know you were a good husband
And a good father to your children
And they loved you till today.
So we have come together
Not to mourn,
But to celebrate your life.

But then one day was the last one,
The way of all human life,
Each one has to leave here
And go through that door alone.
The Book of your life was written
And then the cover was closed.

No one will open that Book again
Except the hand of God alone.
We know you were a child of God,
You came from God,
And to God you have returned.

So back in heaven we pray
That you will share with angels

The joy
That you shared with us each day.
We know that you were a man who knew
How to celebrate life while you lived
So we celebrate your life today.

To Ed Glover,
A man who knew how to live,
And who taught his children well.

December 24, 1985
Sudbury.

POEMS FOR SPECIAL PEOPLE (2): for Archbishop Tutu
I was asked to give the offical welcome to Archbishop Tutu from the Native people of Canada in May, 1986:

PEACE WARRIOR

It is an honour and a pleasure
To greet you, a peace warrior,
A man whose life is dedicated
To peace and justice on the Earth.
We are brothers in the same struggle,
Peace Warriors.
Your dedication is to peace and tranquillity
on the Earth,

And, as Dr. Alan Boesak said:
"If there is no justice,"
There can be no peace.

I remember those women and men
Like Winnie
And Nelson Mandela
And Steven Biko
Whose lives were, and are
Dedicated, and lived, and devoted to the struggle
For justice in the Black Homeland.
I pray for and I expect to see that day come
very soon.

I will not forget you, ever,
Because your struggle and your work
Are my struggle and my work too.
There is only one enemy of peace
In all the Earth,
Just as there is only one God
Of all Creation.

I want to say to you:
Brother,
Welcome to this sacred land.
And my prayers will always
Go with you
And with my Black Sisters and Brothers
In their Sacred Homeland
Until peace is won.

Kitchi Meegwetch.

THE TREE OF LIFE THAT DIED IS LIVING AGAIN TODAY

They said that a long time ago
There lived a holy man of the Sioux Nation,
His name was Black Elk.
He lived many years on this sacred land.
Before he died, he was given a vision of what was to come,
What would happen to his people,
And they said that the sadness that came
To his heart from that vision
Was what killed him.

He saw the desolation that would come to the Earth
And to his people.
In his vision Black Elk saw the Tree of Life,
A Tree that is not visible to human eyes;
The Tree was withered and dying
Right down to its roots.
He said, " I see you there, by those grey shacks
Sick and diseased and dying
And I see that life will be very hard for you."
They said he prayed to God not to let it happen,
He even offered his own life even though he was then
Very old,
But the vision was true,
And the destruction and desolation
Came to the land and to the people.
>   *But we are the keepers of the land,*
>   *not the owners.*
>   *Because we cannot own*
>   *what belongs to God.*
We have stood strong, strong
Against the onslaught of progress and development
Against governments and corporations.
Through the centuries we warned against fouling the water
And the air and the Earth,

But no one listened to us
And the destruction continues.

On July 8 this year, 10,000 Navajo people
Will be forcibly relocated
From their homeland at Big Mountain, Arizona,
By the United States military.
For the Navajo it is their sacred homeland
And they will die if necessary
But they will not move.

Why is this happening?
Because under that land, there is oil,
There is coal, there is water, and there is uranium,
And the giant corporations
Want to get into that storehouse of treasures
And the people must go.

Ten years ago the corporations got the U.S. government
in Washington
To declare the Navajo homelands
A national sacrifice area.
A public law was passed accordingly,
Which on this coming July 8
Will be enforced by the United States military.

Have you heard the words
Justice?
Freedom?
Democracy?
Fair Play?
And did you perhaps hear the words
"Thou shalt love thy neighbour as thyself"?

But the cries of God's children for justice
Are being heard
And there will be a day of accounting.

We have stood,
And we still stand strong,
Against injustice
And against prisons
And against the desecration of the Earth
And the people of the Earth.

It must be obvious,
That at no time in the history of the human family
Has the Earth been so desecrated
And fouled up as it is now,
And now we face the two greatest imperatives
That have ever been seen on the Earth,
And they are:
Either we destroy the environment until
It can no longer support life
Or we will have a nuclear holocaust.

But, we have the power within us to stop both —
So the question now is:
Do we have the vision and do we have the will?
Life was not given for us to endure, but to celebrate, together.

Did you know that the World Council of Churches
Has said that:
" The Native spiritual ways are among
The great faith traditions of the world"
And that they need to come and learn from us.
They will do that here in Canada in 1987.
And did you know that the United Church of Canada
Will make
A national act of contrition
Here in Sudbury this summer in August, 1986
To the Native people of this country?

I have been involved in the struggle for justice
For more years than I can remember,

And I am again reminded of Dr. Alan Boesak,
When he said,
If there is no justice,
There will be no peace on the Earth.
It is that simple.

I have been convinced for many years
That God is not going to allow
God's creation
To be destroyed by the hands of fools.
And I have never been so affirmed and so certain
Of the future as I am now because,
We have the power within us
To heal this sick and troubled world;
It is the most powerful medicine
That was ever given
And the name of that medicine is L.O.V.E.
And, there are many across the world
Who have the courage and the will to use it,
And they are changing the world, right now
While we sit here.

And the simple truth is:
That as we heal others,
Our own healing comes to us,
Only in that way can there be peace and tranquillity
On the Earth.

Yes, the Tree of Life *is living*
And will come into full bloom again
Because there are those among us
Who refuse to let it die.

Kitchi Meegwetch.

> *Presented as a Convocation Address to the graduating class*
> *of Laurentian University, Sudbury, June, 1986.*

A PRAYER TO THE CREATOR

Art Solomon, Ojibway, sends out his voice to the Creator —

Divine Creator
We understand that you are the supreme craftsman, the one we call the first worker.

You are the one that has put this world together for us, and you are the one that keeps it together so that everything is good.

We thank you for the grass and the strawberries and all the medicine plants.

We thank you for the small bushes and the trees and we see that they are still following your original instructions about how they should do their work.

We thank you for the air that you gave us to breathe and for providing for it the way to clean and renew itself.

We thank you for the bird life and for their songs; we thank you for giving them their original instructions how they should do their work.

We thank you for the water that we drink and clean ourselves with. We thank you for the fish life that you put in that water and that you made the water clean and good so your children could be happy.

We thank you for our brothers and sisters and that you made this earth such a good place for them to live.

We thank you for our mother the earth and that she is still following your original instructions to her.

We thank you for the stars, that they are still doing their work even though we no longer understand what it is.

We thank you for our grandmother the moon that we call the night sun. We know that you gave her a great power to raise the great salt water and to regulate the female life so that she controls when the children will be born.

We thank you for the faces of the ones who are still coming towards us and we understand that we are supposed to keep this earth clean and good for them, and that we are to put no fence and mark no places where they cannot go.

We thank you for the fire that you gave us to use in our lodges.

We thank you for our elder brother the sun, that he gives us light and that he still follows your original instructions.

We thank you for the thunder beings that speak to us with your power and your voice from the spirit world.

We know that you have given work to other beings of the spirit world to watch over us to see how we take care of our mother earth and her other children.

And we know that if we followed your original instructions to us and shared your gifts with our brothers, we would not see the big troubles that are in the world today.

ONEH

NATIVE SPIRITUALITY

ON NATIVE SPIRITUALITY

*To try to describe Native spirituality is like trying to talk
about the Earth Mother and the myriad life forms that are
contained within it, but I will try.*

First of all I need to say
that I have to speak about life;
I have to say that in its vast complexity
is its profound simplicity.

Second.
The God that I pray to is totally
male and totally female,
and it is within that totality,
that completeness, that ecstasy,
that God is.
We as Native nations have never had
a definition for God as a totally male god.
We prefer to speak of the Creator
as the life force, which is within all
things that live, whether trees, or
animals or birds or fish or whatever.

Native spirituality is a way of life.
It's not something that we talk about.
It's a way to live constantly.
It is a way of thanksgiving for life.
First of all to the Creator God
for giving us life for another day.
To our Earth Mother for providing
the food that we need to keep healthy
and strong to do the work that we
need to do each day.

We recognize that we need to give
thanks to our Elder Brother Sun

for continuing to do his work
according to his original instructions.
And we give thanks also to our
Grandmother Moon for her work
of regulating all the female life
on the earth. Her work is to take care
of all the female life in the creation:
when the fish life has to be renewed,
each in their own time;
when the animal life has to be renewed.
The work of our Grandmother Moon
is fertility. She decides when women
will have their babies to renew
and replenish the human species.
We give thank for the Star World also
though we know so little anymore about their work
except for guidance at night.

We give thanks also for the spirit helpers
who have chosen to give us their help and guidance.
We give thanks for the plant life,
for the animal life.
We give thanks for the fish life.
We give thanks for the water and the fire
and the medicines
and for the air that we breathe
We give thanks for the Thunder Beings
And for the water that they bring
to replenish the life on this planet.

We give thanks to the Earth Mother
for the sacredness of her work,
without which life would not be possible
for us here in this part of creation.

THE SWEAT LODGE

The sweat lodge is a form of individual and collective purification for those who participate in it. It has been a sacrament that was pretty well universal across Canada and the United States.

It had to be hidden for many years because Native spiritual practices were forbidden by law by the governments of Canada and the U.S.A., while the missionaries did their deadly work of Christianizing us to their various ways of belief and practices. Remember we were told for years that we were savages and pagans and our souls had to be saved only through Christianity. In the sweat lodges we rarely prayed for ourselves, but for each other, for the water, and for the whole creation. We gave thanks to the grandfathers who came in the hot rocks — each one individually. We made offerings of cedar and sage to them and greeted them as they came in.

We gave thanks for their power. For we recognized them as the oldest created things on the earth. When they came in red hot in a very small enclosed space, they had a lot of power indeed.

It is not anyone who can do a sweat, but only those who have been taught over a very long period of time, usually for years. Sometimes there are spirits who come in and show themselves visibly or in the form of sound or light, so it is a serious business. (It is not a sauna.)

There are usually four rounds. There is a very definite pattern to the work of running a sweat. There is one leader and sometimes a helper. Women usually do sweats for women and men do sweats for men. Sometimes there are mixed sweats but there are those who choose not to do mixed sweats or do them only reluctantly.

The sweat lodge ceremonies are coming back again. They can be done at anytime. Sometimes a person who has the authority to do them would have to do three or four sweats in one day and perhaps many times in one week. No one gets paid to do a sweat, but a person who requests a sweat is expected to offer some tobacco and perhaps some cloth of various colours. Normally a sweat keeper or a sweat holder will announce a time when he is going to do a sweat and invite people to come if they want to.

FREE WILL

We recognize that every human person is given a free will and that is so precious that not even the Creator God will interfere with that in any way whatever, because if he/she interferes with that then it is no longer free will.

However, the Creator God has unlimited ways to communicate with God's children and usually it is through helper spirits. So it up to us to keep those channels open.

And because that free will is so precious, we will not say to another person that they have to follow the way that we do. We will share with them and show them and help them if they ask us, but never interfere with their right to choose their own way, even if it is another faith tradition.

THE VISION QUEST

The vision quest was undertaken by a young boy
or a young man to find his purpose in life
and to ask for spirit helpers or spirit guides
to guide him through his lifetime so that he could
walk in a good way, respectful and honourable
and humble.
The young boy normally fasted for four days
and four nights totally alone
he would normally ask a grandfather or
a medicine person to help him.
He might be given a dream or dreams
or a spirit visitor might come
in the form of an animal or a bird
or perhaps in the form of light,
and he would need help in trying to interpret
the possible meaning
that was the reason for asking
an older person to help.

For the little that I know
a young woman did not have to go on a vision quest
as a young man did.
At her first menstruation a lodge was built
for the young woman
where she spent several days
where the older woman spent time teaching her
about the meaning of a woman
and the purpose of her life
which consisted of many, many things
more than just having babies.
And when the young woman came out of her lodge
she was dressed up as pretty as possible by the older women
and there was a feast and a celebration
in the community.

It was our women who kept
the harmony and the balance
in the community.
And they were the first teachers of the language
and the culture and the ways of the people.

A WARRIOR

The warrior had the responsibility to help the people
with whatever they needed,
to go out and hunt so there was food
for everyone, especially the old ones who could
no longer hunt for themselves,
because we had no old age homes.
We did not need them.

When there were problems the laws
of right and wrong were written
in the hearts and minds of the people.

Justice, when it had to be done,
was always tempered with mercy.
It was all the people together who debated
what had to be done.

The clan system was our government
and everyone had an equal say
even those who dissented.
We had to talk things out patiently
until everyone agreed on a course of action.

The warriors were the ones who helped the people
and protected the people when that was
necessary.

Women were always respected.
They had an equal voice with men.
Men listened whenever women spoke
they were not subordinate in any way
that way there was no imbalance
in our relations.

What I say here is not to be construed
as Bible truth, or as the only way that our people
see or live their spirituality.
This is only intended as a guide
or as a window to see how our people
went about their lives.

The sacred pipe was given to our people
As a means to pray with it.
It was brought by a woman
from the spirit world.
The pipe does not belong to the pipe carrier
but to the people
and it is to be used for the people.

The sweet grass is used for purification,
normally before a ceremony,
the sage and the cedar are used for the same purpose.
As well
the sacred tobacco is used to pray with.
It has been said
when you pray and you offer the sacred tobacco
I will see your prayers
in the smoke of the tobacco.

THE SUNDANCE, ALSO CALLED THE RAIN DANCE IN WESTERN CANADA

I know very little about these dances
since they are only beginning to come back
to our part of the country (Ontario).
I have only participated in one in Alberta
and the rule is, as I understand it,
that a person is required to dance in a series of four
that would take four years.
In the sundance men have their skin cut open
and a leather thong
tied to their chest in two places
or on their backs behind the shoulders.
In the case of the back the thongs are tied to a buffalo skull
and the dancer has to dance until the thong
breaks through the flesh.
In one case a little boy was asked to sit on the skull
before the thongs broke from the dancer.
In the matter of thongs tied to the chest
the other ends are tied to the sundance tree
which is standing in the centre of
the sundance lodge.
It is a tree cut especially for the purpose
and dug into the ground.

At the sundance that I attended in Alberta
or raindance as it might be called
no one pierced but remarkable things happened there.
We danced for four days and four nights
without food or water.
We danced where we stood, no one moved from where
they were placed.
If for some reason someone had to go somewhere
they had to ask someone to dance in their place
until they came back.

After the singing stopped
we simply lay down on the ground
where we had danced all day
no blankets, no nothing.
At sunrise we started again
there were only hand drums used for the singing
and there were many singers.
One would sing for what seemed like hours
then another and another.
On the fourth day the singing stopped
We left the lodge a short ways
and we sat on the ground to eat food
that had been prepared for us.
When we had finished eating there was a giveaway
that went on for about one and a half hours.
Many gifts were given to the dancers.
One of the remarkable things
that happened before in preparation,
the medicine man asked his friend and helper
to come with him to go find a place.
So they went to a likely place
they sat down on the ground
they smoked a sacred pipe
and immediately
there came a rainbow close to where they sat.
They finished smoking and refilled the pipe again
immediately they began to smoke the pipe,
the rainbow returned again.
That's how the site was chosen.

There were a number of sessions
the previous winter and spring
for practice singing sessions
that went on for hours into the night.

The reason for all this sacrifice and dedicated work
was to pray for *all the people*, for the Earth Mother,
and to give thanks to and for the whole creation.
We do not spend our time asking for things
But rather giving thanks for what we already have.

Native spiritual ways are for sharing
with others, they are not for sale.
There are those people who make a living
Out of selling what they call
Native spiritual practices.
They do great harm to everyone.
We call them bogus medicine people.
We need money for travel and food and accommodation
and we need money for other things
but it is not our purpose to make a living
out of helping and teaching our sisters and brothers
who are in need of help.

The highest level that I can reach is to be
a helper and I am satisfied with that.
I am not a medicine man.

"SE' TSE EH" — GRANDFATHER

May we hear your breath of life in the winds.
May the shrill cry of our relative, the Eagle,
intercede on our behalf.
Mee-gwetch, you have given us the four sacred
directions.
We would restore what greed has taken from the earth.

SE' TSE EH

Take pity on us this day
for we are weak.
Open your eyes in us
that we may see.
Open your ears in us
that we may have compassion and understanding
upon the earth, our Mother —

SE' TSE EH

May we walk in balance
and our hearts and minds be swift
to honour and protect the earth —
May we learn the lessons
from the plants, the air,
the waters and Council Fires.
May our strength restore her —

SE' TSE EH

When we face our brother, the sun,
in the west —
When we come singing the AIM song —
that warrior song,
may our drum, like the heart beat of the woman,
lift our spirits

— without guilt
— without self-humiliation
— without self-pity
For we are all brothers and sisters on the land.

"Se' tse eh" means "Grandfather" in the Mohawk language.

SPIRIT HELPERS

There is a purpose and a meaning for every human life; it is given at the moment of conception by the Creator God. There is not only a purpose and a meaning for every human life, but there is also a destiny and the power to accomplish that destiny. And there is also a free will given to each child of God. That free will is so special and so precious that not even the Creator God will interfere with it, otherwise it is no longer free will. However, the Creator has unlimited ways to communicate with us, we can call them Guardian Angels or Spirit Helpers or whatever.

Each human being is first a spirit entity within a human body. The Spirit entity is from God, the human body comes from the earth. In dealing with a human being we have an obligation to recognize that we are dealing with two separate entities, spiritual and physical. To try to deal with the physical without recognizing the spiritual entity is not enough. It is like putting a band-aid on cancer.

I once saw a frog with his both hind legs in a snake's mouth. I pondered whether to take the frog out and let him free again and whether he would still have his hind legs to get around with. As I stood there I realized there were no kind words that I could say to the frog that would ease his pain or his anguish and his inevitable end. So I walked away and let the inevitable happen.

I told that story at a meeting of psychologists who were debating how to help young Native people with psychological problems. What they seemed unable to see or understand was that their patients were being *devoured from within* so to speak. The psychologists seemed unable to understand the dynamics of the realities of what we as Native people have to live with. We understand and deal with the world that we live in on two levels: the intellectual, with our minds, and on the soul level; or on the superficial and the real as it were. Those young people understood on the subconscious level that their inheritance *had been stolen from them*, by compulsory miseducation, by the politics of the education system. And by what I call a wage slave economy which all of us are caught up in whether we realize it or not.

You cannot give what you do not have. In other words you cannot teach what you don't know. The teachers taught what they knew but of the purpose and the meaning of life they knew nothing. So therefore it was *compulsory miseducation*.

In our Native ways of teaching nothing is left out so a person comes out *a whole person prepared to accomplish their destiny whatever that may be.*

Native children have been taught for centuries that their people were no good. They were savages. They were killers. They scalped people. They were drunks. They were lazy. They were no good for nothing. Every child was taught that way, not just the Native children, so it became institutionalized racism and everyone from the top to the bottom was infected with the disease of racism. We as a people here in the Western hemisphere have come through the worst and the longest holocaust ever inflicted in the history of the human family. But we have survived. That was done by those who insisted that they were Christian and civilized.

So is it so surprising then that our young people commit suicide at such an appalling rate? There is a Native community that lives 100 miles from where I live. There were eight suicides in one week, plus about thirty attempted suicides at the same time. A sweat lodge was done that summer, the first time in about one hundred years. During that sacred ceremony one of the young people who had committed suicide came back and he spoke to the people in the lodge. He said:

"The reason that we have chosen to end our lives is because when we looked back into our past, there was nothing there, and when we looked ahead into the future, there was no future either, so we ended our lives."

What it meant was that when they asked their old people about the past their old people could not tell them about the past because they had been Christians for more than one hundred years. When they asked about the future of Native people in this land they could not see a future. The young people saw no purpose and no meaning for their life so they ended their lives.

SPIRIT WINDS

I've never been more certain and
more affirmed
as when I got on the plane in Nairobi.

I had been to the Fourth Assembly
of the World Conference on Religion and Peace.

And after I got on the plane
I realized — well,
it was just given to me like a dream, you know.

I was more certain and more affirmed
than I have ever been
and I have described it as
a Great Spirit Wind
that is moving across the earth
all the whole world
and gathering speed and power
as it moves along.

And that comes from the hearts and minds
of people who are saying we don't need
any more war. We need
peace and tranquillity
on this earth.

And that's the affirmation that I was given.

EATING BITTERNESS

BLASPHEMY

Surely it must be the highest form
of blasphemy
to have to live a life without meaning
and purpose
yet walk in the sight of God
on this earth.
I guess all I can say is
       Oppressor, beware.
Because the day will come
when the author
and sustainer
of all life
will come,
and you who stole
the purpose
and meaning
of life
from
his children
will
pay
the price
for
    your
       stealing.

A HEALING WAY

There comes a time when we must stop crying
and wringing our hands and get on with the healing
that we are so much in need of.

Our people are crying in our communities;
there are broken families —
and every kind of disaster afflicts us.
A good doctor would see that someone is sick
and would work not only at healing the sickness,
but would look also at the cause of the sickness —
when you remove the cause, there is no more sickness.

A Brazilian educator, Paulo Freire
said that you have to denounce, announce, and go beyond.
If you're going to denounce, then you have to understand
what it is you're denouncing
before you can announce;
when you've announced, you've said
what you're going to do about it.

You can't begin your journey
until you've gone through this process.

If you would give me a brush with black paint,
I would write on the wall the reason for the problems
in our families and in our communities.

I would write one word: oppression.

I know some of the things I say will be hurtful
to some of our brothers and sisters —
but if we have to go through an operation,
then there are things that will be hurtful
in order to take out what is wrong
and begin the healing process that we are so much in need of.

There is a need for humility —
not only among us, but among the strangers who came to us.
I've puzzled for many, many years
for the answer to the question:
> *Why is it that the strangers were allowed to come*
> *to this sacred Island?*

They have desecrated not only this sacred Island
and everything that is here — but the people as well.
I constantly think of the magnificent gesture of the strangers
who came, stole our land —
and gave us the little reserves we live on.
They forgot that only the One
who created the world can say, "I own this."

The answer to the question came from a group of Elders.
The answer was simple and there were two parts to it:

We had left our ways behind, the ways given us by the Creator
It was a simple way — but a way with a strong discipline;
these people were then sent as a punishment —
and they did it with a vengeance.

The second part is this: they came to learn from us —
because if you see things clearly now,
we are the teachers, we are the leaders.

When the newcomers first came, they said:
> *'We have all the answers that you could possibly need.'*

The mistake that they made
was that way back in their own history,
they dispensed with the most fundamental laws of creation
by which all things work in harmony.
They set aside these fundamental laws —
and made their own laws.

What differentiates us as Native people
from those people is a difference in philosophies.
The philosophy they came with was based on
was the false concept of materialism.

Each of us is gifted,
Everyone of us is gifted — and the tragedy
for so many of our young
is that they have never learned that they have these gifts.
That's why we must help our young people.

When others set aside the fundamental laws of creation,
those laws that we live by, we had very little choice;
we depended on the animals, the birds, the fish in the water.
We had total dependence — and we recognized this.

>*We lived recognizing the power, beauty*
>*and sacredness of creation —*
>*and understood that it was our responsibility*
>*to live in harmony with it*
>*to live in harmony with creation.*

We are less than perfect as a people.
There are no people in this world who are perfect.
I've seen a few who come close, and some of them
are white people.
I've seen a few who are living saints;
some I've walked and talked with.

When the fundamental laws of creation were set aside,
an artificial reality was created which they chose to respond to
in a superficial way
and it is that which causes so much pain.
The anguish and pain of men and women is caused
because we are children of the Creator —
and we want the real thing.

We want to be loved.
We need to be loved
Because it is the nourishment of all human beings.
We need to recognize this and even sometimes
be told this by others.

I once met a young woman in prison.
She had gone through the experience of being ripped
from her family when she was a very young child.
Both her parents were alcoholic.
No-one ever told her she was beautiful.
She went from one foster home to another
until finally she was in a foster home where she was abused.
Her only defense was to burn the house down —
and there was a baby in the house who was killed.
At seventeen she was in prison.
As I visited her together with a lovely Mennonite friend,
we could tell that she wanted help,
but she couldn't ask for it directly.
The lovely man I was with turned to her and said:
" God never created garbage.
Inside of you is a very beautiful human being —
the one the Creator made."
It was months before she could even accept that.

What is Christian charity?
What is Christian living?
All of us need to consider that
and ask what it means to us when we encounter someone
in the situation of the young woman in prison.

When the newcomers came to us
with an arrogance beyond comprehension,
they came without awareness of their arrogance.
Their God of worship was a God of materialism.
They spoke about the One who created them —
but they worshipped materialism.

We live in pain for not following the ways that were given to us.
We are being punished for not following those ways.

In our Midewiwin teachings,
we talk about the four sacred colours of people on the earth.
The yellow people have continued to follow their ways.
The red and black people try to follow theirs —
and the white people, a long way back,
had lost the very simple teaching of the Creator;
they had lost their way.

The Creator sent his son to teach them
what is called Christianity,
because they had lost their way.
We accept that we'd never heard about Christ,
about Christianity,
but we lived by it —
and it had to be real for us.

An important part of the Midewiwin teaching
is that there is no hypocrisy
because we are constantly involved
with the spirit world —
and we cannot play games with them.

We live with a threat of nuclear holocaust.

I believe there will not be a nuclear holocaust
and the reason is that God is not going to allow
God's creation to be destroyed by the hands of fools.

We are destroying the earth's oceans.
We are destroying tree life in the Amazon.
The Ozone layer is being destroyed —
and we are destroying ourselves.

There are two ways to destroy: mindlessly and deliberately.
The results are the same either way.

I have said for many years
that before we destroy this creation,
at some point, it's all going to stop.
The One who made it is still in control,
the One who can connect it.

We must think when we're using paper
that it comes from trees — and not waste or misuse it.
We cannot go on accepting the use of plastic.
The mindless destruction of creation must stop;
we are coming into a time of correction.

We are beginning to see storms now;
they are mild compared to what is coming.
We see a drought right across the earth
and our prophets talk about a time when our mother,
the Earth Mother
will find it hard to feed her children.
There will be more hungry.
The corn that used to grow tall will grow shorter and shorter.

One of those prophets talks about a time
when man will build a house in the sky —
and the tops of the trees begin to die;
when this happens the destruction is almost over.
Scientists are now studying why the trees are dying,
We could tell them why — and we could tell them what to do
to correct it.

When we complained about the loud noise and smells
of lumber mills,
they silenced our complaints in the name of
progress and development.
It has another name: death and destruction.
Wherever people have only development and profit in mind,
death and destruction have come to the earth
and the people of the earth.

How long will we laugh in the face of God?

That's exactly what's been happening.
It cannot continue to happen.
Right now, every one of us as individuals
has an opportunity that I have never seen before in my lifetime.
Now is the correction time and we have an opportunity
to be involved.

Our children are crying out to us:
"We want a new world, and we want it now."

They have a right to it.
All of us have that right.
We are the ones who are going to have to make this new world.
We are going to have to learn again
how to respect each other as men and women.
Understanding of respect is one of the strongest principles
held in the belief system of the Native today.

When one considers the apology
which the United Church has extended to Native people,
and considers in what way to respond,
we remember that in the past
wherever we may have gone,
we were never allowed to express ourselves.
In employment, in religion, in just about every way
we were not allowed to be ourselves;
only if we could be like them could we be accepted
and successful.

When someone comes, as the United Church did,
and says they are sorry — that it is time to make room
for our culture and our values, it is time to consider
that our own cultural and spiritual expression is important,
then we must hold this high.

When enough Native people feel good about themselves,
about their beliefs, spirituality and culture,
than we have hope for our future simply because
we may express ourselves according to the way we are.

One day we may share what we believe
and our people will lend understanding in matters of war
and peace;
in caring for the world and environment.
We can lend our understanding of brotherhood and respect,
of caring for family and relationship.

Only in strength can we do this.
We can only make ourselves understood if others
are willing to listen.
Somewhere in the apology is the beginning of something new
for us.

MY RELATIONS: O CANADA

Welcome to this
Sacred Turtle Island.

We are happy to see you
and to welcome you
and to embrace you.

You are our sisters
and brothers from many lands.

And welcome to you also
who call yourselves
Canadians and Americans.

We have a story
to tell you about life.

It begins like this,
We were put here on this land
by the Great Mystery
to be the guardians
and the caretakers
of this part
of the Creation.

We cannot be the owners
of this land
because it belongs to God,

So be welcome to sit with us
and to celebrate life
with us.
We are your hosts.

We understand that
we are spirit beings

who have come
from the Spirit World
and that we must return,
back to the Spirit World.
We are only here for a short
time so we cannot
be the owners of what belongs
to God.

We have watched with great
sadness for a very long time
while strangers came
and desecrated this sacred land
and its people.
It seems that they followed
the ways of a god
who was a stranger
to us.

We are the people
of the earth
who followed the laws
and the rhythm of the Creation.

We saw its power,
and its beauty,
and its sacredness.
And we looked for guidance
and blessing from our old ones
and from the spirit helpers,
so that we would know
how to walk in a sacred way.

Our obligation
was to the unborn
so that when they came
they would find a sacred place

where the meaning and
the purpose and
the sacredness
of life
would be
always in their minds
and their hearts
and in their ways of life.

But the strangers came
and they divided things:
They divided the land,
and they divided the people,
they divided everything
from everything else,
so that now everything
is broken.

And now they cry out
in anguish
for healing
and togetherness
and they seem not to know
where to find it
or what it is made of.

We the original people
of this land,
know the nature
of that healing
and how to use it
because we have never
let go of it;
But we have been
pushed aside,
and like our Brother Wolf
we have been despised

and hated,
Our families have been
torn apart
by laws and lies
and missionaries,
by genocide,
and forced assimilation.
Our men and our women
and our children
are thrown in jail
where the only medicine
that they are given is hate.

O Canada
you are sick.
Yes sick unto death,
because
in the weaving
of your tapestry
you have rejected
and refused,
the most colourful
the most fundamental,
thread of all.
You have refused to include the original
people of this land
and your tapestry
of life will never
be completed.

O Canada
you say there is freedom
of religion,
But for who?
For Christians and Jews
and others yes,
but not for us the Native people

except in hollow words
without meaning.

Who will speak for us?
Where are the Christians?
Where are those who say
they care?

We have stood alone
in the face of the onslaught
of civilization.
Do we still stand alone?
Or are there some who
will speak to those governments
on our behalf,
so that our people in prison
will be allowed the healing
of their own
spiritual ways?

I would remind you
that we lived in this land
for hundreds of thousands of years
and we had no prisons,
we had no police,
and no prison guards.
We had no one to sit
in judgement over anyone,
because we had no prisons,
and we knew
how to live.

We were not put here
for other people
to practice genocide
against us.

God did not intend for us
to be swallowed up
and disappear,
God put us here
for a purpose.

We were here
when the strangers came
and we will be here
for a long time to come.

It will do no good
for you to wring your hands
and sit in your sackcloth and ashes,
because there is no healing in that.

If you want to find
your healing
in this land,
you must learn
that the medicine
is in the teaching
that says,
"Thou shalt love thy neighbour
as thyself."

But you must also understand
that it will not help you
or anyone else
unless you use it.

And the healing
is in the doing,
not in the talking.

If you use it,
we can all begin to heal

including
the original people
of this land.

But you will
have to close your jails
and accept us
and treat us
as Children of God.

And when you stop destroying
the earth
and the people
of the earth
then your healing
can come.

I say to you
who call yourselves Christians
that as long as there are jails
there will be injustice,
and as long as there is
injustice,
there will be
no peace
on earth.

Those who destroy
God's creation,
will be destroyed by it.

"All my relations" is a Lakota formula, somewhat akin to "Amen".

UNIVERSITY EDUCATION

One time I made a cedar bowl.

It came from a knot on a tree,
and I made three bowls.

I gave two of them away and I kept one.

A woman from Montreal came.
She said that's made by machine, you know.
Can't be made by hand.
Got to be made by machine.

But I know I did it by hand.

So she's an expert from Montreal.
It's like a hell of a lot of these people
that came out of the universities, you know.

Educated idiots.

A VERY DIFFERENT WORLD

It's a very different world that we live in today
The generation gap gets wider and wider
In spite of the best that we can do or pray for.
You see the world that we live in is changing very fast,
there's nothing we can do about that
except to try to cope with it as best we can.

This world is heading toward a climax.
it is speeding up day by day.
We are all caught up in a "wage slave economy."
It is a wage slave economy that is different only
in degree from the slavery that was long ago.

The free trade deal between Canada and the US and Mexico
is all about making it *safe for the money*, nothing else;
They plan to create three or four giant trading blocs:
North America, Europe, and Asia which includes Japan
and all of Asia.
There's nothing we can do about that except
to set our hearts and minds against it.
Governments in Canada and the USA are called democratic.
Nothing is farther from the truth. That is a giant delusion.
The real power is somewhere else.
Eisenhower was President of the USA for one term
They tried hard to get him to serve for a second term
but he wouldn't.
After he left off from the Presidency, he was speaking to a crowd
of about 30 thousand people at Dallas, Texas.
One of the things he said was:
"Beware of the military industrial complex".
There was hell to pay after that for about 2 weeks but people
quickly forgot
and things went on as before.

In Canada there are about 8 families who control this country,
I call them the invisible government who really call the shots.
That's how it has always been in Canada.
What we have is *Criminal, Captive, State Governments*
who do what they are told by the elite.
France went through about 36 governments
after the second world war.
A newspaper reporter was sent to Baron Rothschild
to interview him,
he was an exceedingly rich man.
The reporter asked:
"What do you think of the present government?
And the political turmoil in France?"
Rothschild said: "Give me control of the banks of France
and I don't care what government is elected"
To him governments were irrelevant because
if you control the money . . . that's all that matters.
What it means is that politicians can play their games
and pretend
but it doesn't matter all that much.

We are reading the world around us *on two levels*;
on the intellectual level *with our minds*
and on the *subconscious level* or *the soul level*.
We are doing both simultaneously whether we realize it or not.
Our young people are doing the same.

Every child of God is given a destiny and the power
to accomplish that destiny
at the moment of conception by the Creator God.
The power to accomplish that destiny has been stolen by
the Multinational and Transnational Corporations
because the holiest thing on this earth is *The Money*.
Nothing else matters, not human rights. not even human life.

The great negative power the Destroyer is trying to destroy
this creation through destroying individuals, that is people

by creating confusion in the minds of people and
by establishing false principles.
It is not God that has messed up the world as we see it today.
It is people, *human* people.
That is why there has to be a divine intervention.
We have for years called that the purification, when this will
all be stopped and everything will be made
new and beautiful again
as it was when the strangers came here from Europe.
It was a paradise and they turned it into a living hell.

Someone once said long ago:
"Whom the gods would destroy, they first make them insane".
Well, that's the kind of world that I live in now.
It is a fool's paradise.

I was about 9 years old at the Residential school in Spanish
we were out playing at recess
the bell rang for us to go back in to class
I was standing near a fence,
on the other side was beautiful brown earth
that had not been used for planting yet.
I jumped the fence and I stood on that brown earth
facing the sun.
The thought was put into my mind:
"I wonder if I am going to live into a very strange time?"
That could have been called a vision but I saw nothing,
I climbed back over the fence and I went on into class upstairs.
No one apparently noticed that I was late because no one said
anything.

But I certainly noticed that strange new time as it has
manifested itself more and more as time goes on.
I said to myself in 1929 that the music and the dancing
would get more crazy as it went along, so look at it now.
They are always looking for new music and new dances
The more insane the more they go for it . . . why?

Because the vast majority seems have rejected the fundamental
principles on which life is based and they have accepted
the trifles and trinkets instead and
because they have accepted that,
that will be their inheritance.

Our young people are fast discovering now that those trifles
and trinkets have no validity,
they have no meaning and no purpose,
that is why so many of our young people are committing suicide.
They have not discovered that there is a purpose
for each human life.
Their parents long ago abdicated their own responsibility
and there has been a gradual degeneration of the quality of life
for every one.

Our young people inherently know
somewhere in their subconscious
that they have a right to claim their inheritance.
But what is it? Where is it? Where are the guiding principles?
Who can tell them? And who will they listen to?
They know inherently that they are not the ones
who have messed up the world like it is.
It is the ones before them, they can point to us
and say it's them who did it. They stole our future.
It's true we have to take our share of the blame but
the real culprits go unscathed because they are invisible,
whereas we are visible, we are present, they can point to us
but they cannot point to what they cannot see and do not know.

I believe that the greatest imperative that we have
as the indigenous people of this land
is to heal ourselves
and to heal our communities
and to heal our nations
because we are the final teachers in this sacred land.

What we have to teach others is how to live in harmony
with the creation. Men living in harmony with women.
The first man and the first woman were created in harmony
and we were intended to live that way forever, into infinity
it is true that none of us will ever be perfect
as long as we live in these human bodies.
Our work here on this earth is to work at our perfection
as best we can,
> *So that when we have to return to the spirit world*
> *from where we came*
> *we will be able to answer the question:*
> *What have you done with the time, and the opportunities,*
> *and the gifts that I gave you?*
Each one of us is gifted in different ways
It is our responsibility to discover those ways
Some of us do and some us don't.

Because of compulsory miseducation and the politics
of the education system, the vast majority of people
come out confused and disoriented.
Because "you can't give what you don't got".
If students were taught the meaning and the purpose
for their own lives, they would not come out into the real world,
"stunned" to repeat the words of a young girl in an enquiry of
education done in Ontario about 20 years ago.
Education could be vastly different if those who teach
would let it be what it could be.
Learning how to count numbers and how to compete is what
is considered important,
not caring and sharing and co-operating with others.
The churches without exception taught
"Thou shalt love thy neighbour as thyself"
But living it and talking about it are two different things.

> *They came in violence*
> *they have lived in violence*
> *and they will go in violence*

but it will not be the violence of
the aboriginal people of this land
for remember that the God of Creation said:
"Do not take revenge, because revenge is mine alone and I
will repay."
We are a gentle and patient people
We have waited a long time . . . five hundred years
But we will get justice in this land!

At the first international Indian Treaty Conference
quite a few years ago in the United States
There was a French anthropologist from France,
his name was Robert Jaulin.
He said of his own society:
"We are a civilization of vultures and parasites, and we will end
up eating our own decaying flesh."
It has taken me a long time to understand what he meant,
but when I see people in the prisons of North America
and see hundreds of thousands of people hungry and dying
on the streets, I understand.

July 29, 1983, Vancouver

HEALING OURSELVES

I believe that healing for us as human beings will be hard to do
unless we become humble and honest and straightforward
in all our dealings with women and children and men.
What we are searching for is harmony and balance again.
The way that it was before the strangers came to this sacred land,
and messed things up for us with their strange ways.
They came with an unbelievable greed and arrogance.
They came to a paradise and they turned it
into a living hell upon earth.
As Willfred Pelletier said many years ago in Thunder Bay;
"If there is a heaven and hell, Aboriginal people should
be able to go straight to heaven when they die,
because they have already spent a lifetime in hell."

What differentiates us from them is a difference in philosophy.
One is based on the false principle of materialism.
The other is based on the principle of the beauty,
the sacredness,
the harmony and the balance of the creation within which
we were to live.
We did not kill for sport,
we had to kill for sustenance.
We understood that we did not create the animals, the birds
and the fish.
They were created by the God of all creation.
And thus they belonged only to God
and we had to be constantly grateful for that bounty
as well as to the animals whose life we had taken.
Is it wrong for us to live that way?
We have always been a simple people
but for that they have hated our guts.

Yet they had a commandment that says,
"Thou shalt love thy neighbour as thyself."
So how do we heal ourselves?

How did we get unbalanced?
Well the imperative for me is that we as men have to
go back to the old ways again to look back at how we did it
before when there was harmony
in our families and in our communities.
One of the dynamics of life that I have observed
through the years
is the dynamics of tension.
If two or more people come together
there is tension.
It is good or bad,
but there is tension.
It is either positive or negative.
We either like the other person or we are wary.

If we look back into the past we will see that women were
honoured and were respected for who they were
and what they did. There was harmony.
Our women kept the harmony and the balance in the families
and in the communities just by being there.
They taught the language and the customs and the ways
of being and doing.
They were *the glue that held it all together*
in the most beautiful way.

August 3, 1992

THE CHILDREN'S AID SOCIETIES

After the devastation of the residential schools
came the Children's Aid Societies
with their unbelievable arrogance.
They were given the power over families
and the right to take children from their fathers and mothers
regardless of circumstances.
The people were forced into impoverishment,
by governments, by compulsory miseducation and by
the politics of the education system,
by every device possible to discredit us as a people,
by racist attitudes that were and still are
rampant in Canada and the United States of America.
It is illegal for anyone in Ontario
to steal or take the young
of animals or birds, but it is legal
for the Children's Aid Society
to steal children from their mothers
and their extended families
and then to adopt them out to strangers
of another race of people.
It is called genocide by the United Nations.
But that doesn't matter to the C.A.S.

The God of Creation so loved the world
that *she did not create a Children's Aid Society*.
What she created is men and women and it's to them
that she gave the children.

We had a hostage taking yesterday 100 miles from here
because a C.A.S. worker took a child from its mother.
We do not have to guess who will be punished
in this incident. The mother will likely
have to spend time in jail. . .
where she is now.
Where is the justice?

For years the C.A.S. had full sway in Manitoba.
It has been called "the scoop of the fifties"
because in that province, they scooped
our children by the thousands.
The minister responsible was a woman.
That kind of thing went on for some years
until the Native people got angry and forced
an investigation. The minister was fired from her job
and the people insisted on changing things.
They proposed to create their own Children's Aid Society.
They found out in the process
that there was a pipeline down into the United States
where white people were happy to pay money
to adopt little Native children
perhaps because they were cute.
Meanwhile, the people themselves needed money
to start up their own agency,
but it took approximately two years
to convince the federal and provincial governments
that the Native people could do it
themselves.

The Children's Aid Societies of Canada
in their magnificent arrogance and ignorance
have broken Native families
and scattered Native children
to the four winds.
It was a devious and diabolical scheme that saw
Native children shipped across international boundaries
into other countries with a deliberate policy of silence
that guaranteed that the children would never again
find their parents and blood relatives.
All of this action was covered up with the magnificent lie
That it was "in the best interest of the children."
Almost without exception I have found by going into prisons
over the past 12 years

that the victims of the prison system
have been ripped off from their families
by the Children's Aid Society
and put into one white foster home after another
and end up in one correctional facility after another.
And their anger and their frustration grows
because they have been ripped off
from their rightful inheritance.
Their inheritance comes from God,
not from Governments or institutions.
The anger that our young people have against a totally
unjust system *is the anger of God*
and it will have to be accounted for.

All of this racist arrogance and greed is paralleled exactly
by what has happened to the aboriginal people
of Australia over the past 200 years.

THE CRIMINAL "JUST US" SYSTEM

LAWS AND PRISONS

Somewhere
Many centuries back there were those people
Who set aside the fundamental laws of creation
and made their own laws from which came
the chaos that we live with now.

In the 60s when the flower children
rose out of the ground,
the grown ups said,
"Where did we go wrong?"

When Christopher Columbus landed in North America in 1492
there was not one aboriginal person in prison
because there were no prisons.
There were no prison guards, no police, and no lawyers
and no judges.
We simply did not need them because we had
a vastly better way.
The laws of the people were written in the hearts and minds and
souls of the people.
And justice was tempered with mercy
because each human being was a child of God
which is the essence of all living things on the earth.
We call that power the Creator God or The Life Force,
which is within all living things on the earth
when that power is withdrawn,
there is death.

I have been going into prisons on a voluntary basis.
both federal and provincial for some twelve years.
Now, as a Native spiritual leader,
I have come to a sense of total outrage.
I see the whole Criminal "Just Us" System,
as obscene, a sacrilege in the face of God.

An abomination,
it has nothing whatever to do with justice.
It is simply a mechanism of control
which criminalizes the poor and the oppressed
while it protects the rich and the powerful.
More than 100 years ago someone said,
"The poor people have to obey the law;
But it is the rich people who make the laws."

The robber barons and the merchant princes of past ages
in Europe have not gone away
they are here in Canada
and they are alive and doing very well.
And now with *free trade* they will rape Canada
and the Indigenous people of Canada
just as they have raped the people of other countries
which they then call third world countries.

A society that mindlessly steals the inheritance
of its own children in the name of *progress and development*
can't go very far, it is a society that has no future.
There was an international conference on prisons
held in Toronto September 1987.
The most significant thing that I heard from that conference
came from the Solicitor General of Canada.
He said, "We are going to build a maximum security prison
for young offenders near Ottawa";
Is that the best that Canada can do for its children?
Those who sow the wind will eventually reap the whirlwind.

The notion that prisons solve the problem of crime is insane,
because it solves nothing.
What it does in fact is multiply the evil.
One evil multiplied by another evil is more, not less evil.
In a criminal court it is the state against the individual
and a court of law is the most fearful place to be in.
A criminal court is not a place of justice.

It is a place of judgement where punishment is meted out,
and where mercy has no place,
not for the individual or for the family of the individual.
That is not justice, it is vengeance.

Cameron Curley is a young man from Manitoba
who made the mistake of being born to a Native man
and woman.
He saw his father killed by someone.
Then he saw his house burn down
where he lived with his mother.
The Children's Aid Society
came and took him away from his mother,
in spite of the many pleas of relatives who wanted to take him in
and provide a home for him.
In their infinite wisdom and their arrogance beyond
comprehension,
C.A.S. shipped him to a man in Texas
who was a proven sex offender.
In that man's home was at least one other Native boy
who eventually ran away.
There was a lot of sexual and physical abuse
that both boys lived.
Finally, in desperation
Cameron Curley reported what was happening
to his teacher at school
The teacher reported to authorities and to the police.
But no action was ever taken.
Then one day Cameron Curley picked up a gun
and shot his tormentor dead.
Cameron was sent to prison for life in an American prison.
Eventually there was a request to the government of Canada
to take him back,
which was refused.
Neither country wanted him.

Time went on and we learned that Cameron Curley
was lodged at Stoney Mountain prison in Manitoba.
When I last heard of Cameron a year ago,
The parole board had been dangling him on a string
for some months as they so often do with Native prisoners.

Don St. Germaine was murdered in cold blood
at Kingston penitentiary about three years ago.
Why is murder not a murder when it is committed
by a prison guard
against a defenceless man?
Don St. Germaine had been asking for me to go down to K.P.
to help him that morning.
I could have prevented that murder if they had flown me
from French River where I live,
by float plane to the Bay where K.P. is situated.
It says something for a system that prefers to murder a man
in cold blood,
rather than to do the human thing
and provide the assistance needed.
The prison psychologist at K.P. had called at my home
about 8:30 that morning saying
Don St. Germaine was asking my help but I was
four hundred miles away.
To drive would take eight hours minimum.
But if they wanted to they could have arranged for a float plane
from Sudbury to pick me up at the river
and land me right at the prison.
It would take a maximum of one and a half to two hours
to do that.
There was an inquiry a short time later
and two of my friends were there.
One a Native lawyer and one a Native law student.
As this make believe enquiry was in process
one turned to the other and said,
"I have to go outside and puke, this is so sickening to watch."

All of this was done by a people who profess to be Christians,
two of the commandments say,
"Thou shalt not kill."
and "Thou shalt love they neighbour as thyself."

I have come to the conclusion that
After going into the prisons of Canada for twelve years,
there is nothing so much need of correction
as the Corrections System of Canada.

January 16, 1989

FREEDOM OF RELIGION

For these past eight years the Native spiritual ways
have gone into the prisons in Ontario
as a social thing,
in other words *as a privilege*
not as a right.

Native spiritual ways must go into the prisons
under the established principle of
Freedom of religion
and with the same respect and rights
that are accorded to any other faith tradition.

We are not missionaries now, or never were,
and we never will be
in spite of the statement made by a professor
at Queens University about a year ago where
he classed us as missionaries.

The sweat lodges should not be torn down
after they are used, rather they should have a snowfence
put up around them,
they should only be taken down when they need to be replaced
and only at the discretion of the one who does the sweat.

Do not take away objects that are used to pray with
such as abalone or other sea shells
sweet grass, sage, tobacco, medicinal objects
such as sweet flag roots, etc.

Since the sacred pipe can only be used to pray with
there should be no need for elaborate previous notice
by administration.
It should also be allowed in to solitary confinement
along with sage, tobacco, sweet grass, etc.

The person doing a ceremony is totally responsible
for all aspects of that ceremony,
no one unless delegated by the *celebrant*
has any say in who will handle the sacred elements.

I heard it said at P4W when Edna Manitowabi
did a sweat there in September this year,
that it would be OK for the Native sisters
to have a sweat twice a year.
If that is so then we feel that it should be OK
for other faith traditions to have their services
twice a year also.
We wouldn't object if they got the same treatment
as us.

To me it is incredible beyond belief
that the prison system in Canada
can afford to pay for the services of chaplains
of the mainline faith traditions
but nothing for Native spiritual leaders
or medicine people and pipe carriers,
in fact there have been a lot of incidents
of very bad treatment, such as recently at Joyceville.
Yet we are told that this country is democratic,
that it is Christian and civilized
I don't know what such treatment says to you
but it sure says a lot to me,
my mildest form of response is to call it
a screaming disgrace.

Native children, our most valuable resource are still
being taken into protective custody (kidnapped)
by both provincial and private child welfare agencies,
and adopted out into non-Native homes
and environments, often losing touch and contact
with their home, family, and culture.
The depriving of a people of their culture, language,

and religion and the taking of children from their
culture is considered to be an act of genocide
by the Geneva convention on genocide at the
United Nations, December of 1948.

This is one of the major reasons why so many of our people
are in jail now.
If you sow the wind . . .

A GRIEVANCE

A short time ago Paul Bourgeois
went into Joyceville to visit the Native brothers
and to pray with the sacred pipe.
On his way in he met with a most incredible harassment by the
prison guard on duty.
Roy Johnson was going in with Paul,
the guard took the pipe in his hands and blew through it
and also did various other things
that were extremely embarrassing to Paul.
It was clearly intended to embarrass Paul as much as possible.

Paul was extremely sick when I talked with him a week later in
Sudbury so I was not able to get details from him
and in any case he was much too embarrassed
to talk about it anyway.
The last words of that particular guard were,
"We are not going to have any of that kind
of bullshit around here."
Roy said that the other guard who was there
tried to dissuade the one who was being
so extremely obnoxious.
That is an obvious case of racist hatred.
My question is,
Who is going to do anything about that kind of
treatment towards us whose only purpose
in going into those places is to help our own people?

I have often run into virtually the same kind
of treatment in going into that same prison.

There should be a special dispensation of time
to accommodate the availability of a Native
spiritual Leader, sometimes from far away,
in relation to periods of prayer
with brotherhoods or sisterhoods.

Because of long distances and costs of travel
and accommodation
It would take me 10 days or more to make one round of the
prisons in Kingston area because of meeting times at each
institution. I live four hundred miles away
and my time is too valuable for me to waste
sitting in Kingston waiting to get in to see the brotherhoods,
plus there has been no money for anything during
these past eight years (except from Nov 15 '82 to March 31 '83.)

Paul Bourgeois asked me to mention that he was treated
with respect
at P4W and Warkworth during the same week
that he was mistreated so badly
at Joyceville.

A LETTER ON BEHALF OF "MARY"

My request is very simple.

I am requesting that "Mary" be released from prison to us at Newbery House in Sudbury as soon as possible where there are many supportive people like myself in what we call a *Healing Community*. She will have opportunity to study in university or to work in the community with us; to participate in the Midewiwin Ceremonies as they happen, (there are four major ceremonies throughout the year), a Children's Survival Camp, and various other projects that we are involved with. She is presently involved in a carpentry course at Collins Bay Institution, and has through the years at P.4.W. taken advantage of every opportunity for education and self improvement.

I have worked some nine years with "Mary" helping her with her spiritual and personal development, and in the twelve years that I have been going into prison (most of those years at no cost to governments) I have not found a more likely person to succeed on the outside. Especially among people who love her and care about her.

She will not be alone, ever, and she intends to get her son from B.C. and live with us at Sudbury and the surrounding community that we are involved with. If she is out soon enough I want to hire her to work in the Children's Survival camp for which I have gotten money from various countries like Holland and Switzerland and England.

I will have a personal care and regard for "Mary" for the next few years and into the future.

P.S.: There is now a pottery course being offered at Newbery House, it is being taught by Jose Garcia of the Manitoulin School of pottery. Jose is the originator and owner of the Manitoulin School of Pottery which has been very successful and significant over the past 15 years. The course is free to residents of Newbery House.

PRISONS ARE AN ABOMINATION

As a member of the Ojibway Nation and of the aboriginal people of this land, I welcome you to this meeting on prison abolition.

My people have lived on this land now called Canada and America, but which we call the Sacred Turtle island, for a hundred thousand years. We had no prisons, no police, no prison guards, no lawyers and no judges. We did not need them because we know how to live. Yet they said we were savages and pagans.

"Why is it that only "civilized", "Christian" people need prisons?"

Prisons are an abomination. They are a blasphemy in the face of God. I cannot believe that God ever intended for any of her children to be locked up in iron cages behind stone walls.

Prisons in Canada are simply a white racist institution. Their track record is an 80% failure. If a medical treatment were an 80% failure, then it would soon be abandoned. Why do we persist in trying to heal social ills with a prison system that fails 80% of the time?

The very simple answer is: *Thou shalt love thy neighbour as thyself and thou shalt not steal.* When the rich stop stealing from the poor, then the poor will stop stealing from others. But the God most people worship is the God of materialism, not the god of Creation. When the false gods are struck down, then there will be no more prisons.

The death penalty is an even greater abomination. While it was in use in Canada, over half of those executed were people of aboriginal ancestry.

There are those of us in North America who invest our lives in advocating alternatives to imprisonment, but no one will listen to us. There are those of us who believe that there must be peace and tranquillity on the earth and who are willing to pay the price to make it happen, but we are called "terrorists" and "communists".

We are aware of the racism whipped up by the government,

by Hollywood, and by the big business-dominated media, which provides a cover for the corporate plunder of Native lands and Native peoples. We are aware that those whose motto is "to serve and protect" are really concerned with "serving" the rich and "protecting" them from the poor.

There are alternatives to prisons; in fact, there need be no prisons at all. But it takes right living. It takes sharing the gifts of God equally with all of God's children. That is what 11 faith traditions teach, but between the teachings and the living, there seems to be no connecting link.

It seems pointless to propose the abolition of prisons to a society that doesn't want to look at working models that existed in the past and would still work today if they were not prevented by the rich and powerful and their captive state governments.

But we, the indigenous people of this land have survived the onslaught of "civilization", with its prisons and jails. We will continue to survive.

From a welcoming address to the Third International Conference on Penal Abolition, Montreal, June 1987 (reproduced in **Outlook on Justice** *Sept/Oct 1987 Vol.5 No.5)*

GENOCIDE

We have survived the onslaught
of Christianity and civilization and we are still here.
If the earth will survive, the indigenous people
will survive, because we have never willingly
or mindlessly destroyed the earth that we live on.

A system that lives off the avails of human misery
cannot last for very long
and that's what prisons are all about, not about justice.
When Pieter Botha said two years ago
"There has to be law and order,"
the next question is, "Whose law and whose order?"
It was from Canada that South Africa
learned how to establish the evil of apartheid
in South Africa.

We would not have to concern ourselves with crimes
by Native people in North America
if the rich were not allowed to steal from the poor
which is how it has been for centuries.
Crime is caused, it doesn't just happen and as long
as laws are in place to favour the rich against the poor
then crime will multiply.
As it is now the law is more important than the people.

Mahatma Gandhi wisely said that
there is enough in this world for everyone's need.
But not enough for everyone's greed.
What God provided in this world *was for all God's children.*
It was intended to be shared equally.
But some are forced to steal just to keep body and soul together.
No system that is so totally unjust can last for long.

There is a motto on some police cars in this country
that says, "To serve and protect."

But if it was written as it should be,
it would say "To serve the rich and protect them from the poor."

The rich are never criminalized like the poor
and the dispossessed
for making the same mistakes.
For instance, an Ontario provincial policeman
pulled over a highly placed official of International
Nickel doing 120 miles an hour in a sixty mile per hour zone.
The policeman gave him a ticket for speeding
which the man proceeded to tear up
saying you might as well do the same with yours.
The policeman gave in his report at the end of his shift,
and next morning on his desk was an unsigned note saying,
"Lay off."
An ordinary citizen would have had no choice but to pay the fine.

It has been very clear to us from time beyond memory
that there is a law for the rich,
there is a law for the poor, and
there is a law for Indians.

Another example is that last summer at Sault St. Marie
A young man was convicted for the rape of a young woman.
The young man was given 3 or 4 months which he was allowed
to serve on weekends.
The judge said that the young man
was from a very respectable family
and they had already suffered enough because of the crime.

Some years before that, two Native women from Kenora
had broken about $500 worth of windows in a school
at a Native community nearby
One woman was given seven years at the prison for women
in Kingston
and the other woman was given nine years at the same place.
It was only because of the massive outrage

by the national and provincial Native organizations
that the sentences were diminished.
To say that there is no racism in the courts
or the police or the prisons is a lie.
A blatant lie.

It has been very clear to us for centuries
that there is an open season on Indians and black people
in this country as well as in the United States of America.
We have not forgotten that our people
were deliberately given diseased blankets in order to destroy us.
We have not forgotten also that there were those in America
who armed themselves with guns
and deliberately set out to destroy our people
by shooting them down as though they were vermin.
Has the God of Creation forgotten?
We don't think so.

The laws and the policies of the Governments
of Canada through the years has been a deliberate policy
of genocide against Native people which is still going on
despite the protocol against genocide declared by the
United Nations in 1948.

WE DON'T NEED THAT

The language now is assertive.
Totally assertive.

We're saying to the man, "back off."
We've got our way to go.
We have to respond.

At Lubicon Lake, for instance, you know,
the people had nothing stronger
than a guitar and a drum,
and they blocked the road.

So they sent in 50 police, you know,
military guards and armed and everything.
With high-powered machine guns
and that kind of stuff.

We don't need that.

In Quebec they sent in 5,000 military
and 1,500 SQ's, you know.

We don't need that.

We need to negotiate.

But before they can negotiate with us,
they have to accept as full and total
human beings.

A BRIEF TO THE ROYAL COMMISSION ON NATIVE PEOPLE AND THE JUSTICE SYSTEM IN MANITOBA

March 12, 1989

Introduction

Mr. Chairman, I need to begin by telling you that much of the thinking for this brief was done while I was travelling to and from Australia in connection with a conference of the World Council on Religion and Peace held every fourth year. The reason why I share that information is that, for the life of me, I can not reconcile the situation of my brothers and sisters in the prisons of this country except by saying that it is one of the great obscenities of this moment in history.

I know that you would like me to focus attention on the difficulties and divisions within our own Native and Indian communities which contribute to the high rates of incarceration of our people. I'm also sure you want to explore alternatives to the present system of imprisonment.

I will touch on those things, Mr. Chairman. But I need to make very clear at the outset that the primary factors contributing to the rate of incarceration of our people does not lie with the divisions and difficulties in our own communities. As real as those issues may be, there is a more fundamental problem which is not usually discussed in this context.

Refusing to Aid and Abet the Present Obscenity

We can not discuss the problem of Native and Indian people in prison without looking very carefully at the quality of the relationship between the First Nations in Canada and the economic and political structures under which we are all, to a very large degree, held captive.

I appreciate that such a broad viewpoint may seem to be beyond the scope of your inquiry. But if I were to begin from any other vantage point, I would fail my people. Were I to talk about ways to improve the prison system without first looking at how that system serves the socio-economic system represented by the Canadian and Manitoban governments, I am afraid I would do no more than aid and abet the present obscenity.

"Peace, Peace": The War Out There

I would not be here today, nor would I have travelled around the world, if I were not totally committed to entering into a dialogue in pursuit of peace. But when I look at the relationship of our people to the justice system, in Manitoba and across Canada, I am reminded of the prophetic warning against crying, "Peace, peace" when there is no peace.

The justice system in this country can not be understood separate and apart from the economic and political system which it preserves. And when it is viewed in the context of that larger system it appears to have much more "Just Us" than Justice.

There is a war going on out there, Mr. Chairman. How could I come in here and discuss the niceties of a fairer legal system, a greater respect for Native spirituality in the prisons, or an improved parole procedure and fail to mention that there is a war going on ?

The Destruction of Native Communities

There is a community in northwestern Ontario which was being visited by an anthropologist on the regular court day in the spring of 1954. When the court arrived that day there were no cases to be heard. A pleasant visit was had by the visiting judge and prosecutor and the community leaders and everybody went back to their business. Thirty years later, Mr. Chairman, in 1984, the Crown Attorney for that district told a meeting of the Canadian Bar Association that 25% of the community were up on charges.

What happened to that community in those thirty years? How does a community go from a complete absence of criminal charges to a condition in which — allowing for the infirm, the elderly and those too young to get into trouble — most of the village faces some kind of criminal prosecution?

What happened to that community is what has been happening to Anishnabe and Cree and Métis communities in place after place across this country during these past thirty years. It has also been happening to Chipewyan and Dene and Inuit communities in the north. And to MicMac communities in the east. And perhaps also to the different Nations in the interior and along the coast in British Columbia. Without disregard for any of the First Nations in Canada, I can tell you that the whirlwind has struck with a particular force in the mid north across the country, and particularly in the centre of the country, in Ontario, Manitoba and Saskatchewan.

What has happened has been the destruction of the last vestiges of the economic basis of our traditional way of life. The forces which have brought this about are, I trust, sufficiently familiar to the members of this inquiry that I do not need to recite the facts at great length.

I know there are those outside this room who might believe that our traditional economy had all been destroyed many years ago. Certainly, the events a hundred years ago in this province put an end to the practise of roaming across the prairies following the buffalo.

But twenty and thirty years ago there were communities across the north that were very largely self reliant. Because we were self reliant we could expect that our young people would, to a very large extent, follow the examples set by their elders and rooted in the traditional organization and way of life of our communities.

Twenty and thirty years ago we had already faced the experience of three generations of our children being taken off to residential schools with the primary purpose of preventing them from learning the example of their elders. At that time, we already had a massive influx of our people to the cities. It was already clear that there would not continue to be sufficient opportunity in our own communities to avoid the massive outflow of our best and brightest people.

Why then do I raise the issue of this past generation, the last twenty or thirty years? For one simple reason, Mr. Chairman. If peace in the best and most prophetic sense of the word were a goal of this society, then the powers that be would not simply have continued to eat up the land in the same omnivorous way leaving my people to eat bitterness.

Self Government and Indian Conditions

In 1983, we had a report on Indian Self Government from a Committee of the House of Commons of Canada. It said there was no need to review the living conditions of Indian people because so little had changed since the report entitled *Indian Conditions* written five years before. It pointed to the Hawthorn Report a decade earlier and said how little Indian Education had changed in ten years despite repeated calls from parliamentary committees, and even from ministers calling for Indian control of Indian education.

Here we are today looking at the situation of Native people and the justice system in Manitoba. And there are parallel inquiries going on in other provinces. What am I going to tell you that you could not get out of the innumerable reports already written by inquiries before yours?

Criminal Neglect

Somebody said that the difference between careless driving and criminal negligence is when a person backs up and does the same thing again. We need to look at why and how the economic and political structures of this country have, in the thirty years since the Hawthorn Report, backed up and done it again to the Native and Indian peoples across Canada.

If I thought the purpose of your inquiry were to aid and abet the economic and political powers to back up and do it once again to our people I would not be here engaging in dialogue with you. If you fail to address the fundamental causes of the total breakdown of our communities — if you deal only with the surface symptoms and do not look at the repeated signs and warnings of a deeper illness — then, however good your intentions, you will be doing no more than giving aid and comfort to the enemy.

A Global Perspective

Viewed from a world perspective, Indian and Native peoples today fall into two categories: the larger part of our peoples today are displaced persons; the smaller part are warriors.

The displaced people may be found in the cities and in our own communities and in the prisons. What makes them displaced people is not their geographic location but the state of mind to which they have been conditioned by the dominant society.

On Being a Warrior

What makes one person a displaced person and another person a warrior? The warrior is a person who, one way or another, has recovered their sense of identity. Invariably and without exception, the warrior is person who has gone back to their own roots and gotten in touch with the traditions which have sustained our people throughout the generations.

The warrior who is strong enough to keep an identity in the face of all that threatens to destroy us may live in the city today. Indeed, for some it is the best place to be for the moment. It is the place to make a livelihood. If a person's income is enough to keep them out of the slums, they may have a better chance to raise a family in clean and safe surroundings than if they stayed in the community from which they came.

Warriors in Suburbia

Suburbia may not offer us a substitute for an authentic community but it is a place where a few of our people are able to raise their children in safety and security for the moment.

I hesitated, for a moment, to use the term warrior. I remembered the report of the R.C.M.P. some years ago that identified the Red Power movement as the number one threat to the national security of Canada. I could imagine some reporter running out of here to write a story headlined "Native Elder threatens war at inquiry." Even the R.C.M.P. have not been so silly as to repeat that kind of report.

It is not in the nature of a warrior to wage a senseless battle. A warrior is one who is prepared to fight when the time is right and who engages in serving his people in the hope that war can be averted but also in the determination to pull them up out of the mud.

Big Bear in the Global Village

A hundred and two years ago, Big Bear said that *"The time will come when my people will be of great service to this country."*

In the time of the global village we can begin to understand what Big Bear meant. The world is a single living organism. Every people, every nation, large or small is an organ in that larger organism. If we appear different it is because we each serve a different purpose necessary to sustain the life of the planet as a whole.

Our traditional prophecies saw that very well and I want to say more about those prophecies later. Here I want simply to say that discrimination is not separable from the failure to appreciate and value the contribution that each people has to make to the survival and growth of the planet Earth.

The Miner's Canary

A brilliant American legal scholar made a similar observation. Almost sixty years ago, Felix Cohen, who was then the legal advisor to the United States Secretary of the Interior said that "the Indian is the Miner's Canary."

When you look at the general direction of this society today you see that what is happening to Indian and Native people in Canada is not so very different from what is happening to the young people of every kind. What is happening to our people is simply that the same forces are hitting us earlier and harder; and, at the same time, we have the roots and tradition in this land on which to fall back when we are able to pull ourselves out of the mud and to make ourselves into warriors rather than continue to be displaced people.

I do not mean that there is not discrimination in this society, If there were no discrimination this commission would never have been called to conduct the present inquiry.

I do mean to suggest that the perpetuation of poverty in Canada combines with the rape of the land and with attitudes of racial discrimination to make up the fangs and claws of a monster who is hardly likely to "lie down with the lamb" when it has finished devouring our people. The warrior is any man or woman who can endure and help to heal their people in the face of the monster.

Racism and the Perpetuation of Poverty

We can not separate the question of racist attitudes among law enforcement officials from the depredation of the land or the perpetuation of poverty. Last month, shortly after I returned from the World Council, there was a report of a police chief in Toronto who told an inquiry in Ontario that it would take twenty years to develop a multicultural and multiracial police force in the largest city in this country. That police chief said that he believed everything that could be done was being done within the mandate of his force to improve community relations.

Far from exonerating the police, the chief's argument condemns the ministers and legislators who create his terms of reference. He is simply the loyal servant submitting to arbitrary measures.

Leonard Peltier — Nelson Mandela
The Empire on Trial

What then shall we say of the extradition of Leonard Peltier from Canada and the failure of successive governments in this country to seek his return? I do not think there was a single close observer of the situation at the Pine Ridge Reservation in South Dakota who was not aware that the affidavits submitted to the extradition hearing in the Supreme Court of British Columbia supposedly signed by Myrtle Poor Bear, were fraudulent.

Perhaps if we did not have an extradition treaty with the United States under which the Crown Attorney comes to represent the United States as well as Canada the court would have looked more carefully at the arguments put forth on behalf of Leonard Peltier. I will not speculate whether this treaty was a precursor of free trade.

Warriors of all peoples have come to identify Leonard Peltier's name with Nelson Mandela in South Africa because the quality of justice in these two cases is very hard to distinguish. I understand just how hard that association sticks in the craws of many well intentioned people in Canada.

I fully appreciate that we would not have this kind of inquiry if our governments fully endorsed policies similar to those of South Africa. But Canada's declarations of good intentions are not enough to free this country from that kind of association. The road to hell could be paved with such good intentions. And the hottest fires in Hades would be reserved for the would-be leaders who can not see how very thin is the veneer of liberty in this land.

The answer which I need to give to those who will be angered by the comparison of Canada to South Africa is simply this, Mr. Chairman. From where our peoples stand, the policy of apartheid is like murder while the continued practices of Canadian governments is like criminal negligence committed day after day and generation after generation.

The Police and the First Ministers

The attitudes of the police in this society are not different from the attitudes displayed at the First Ministers' Conferences on the entrenchment of aboriginal rights. The quality of attitudes displayed, especially by the federal government in the recent Lubicon negotiations, is only marginally different from attitudes we witnessed years ago.

If anyone seriously doubts the connection between what happens to Native people in the justice system in this country and our socio-economic status, let him stop and consider what the situation would be today if all the widely applauded reports on Indian and Native issues of the past twenty years or so — reports endorsed by our own leadership — had been implemented in a spirit of good will:

- Indian Self Government would be a reality in every Indian community who wanted to take control of their own lives.
- The resources available for those governments would be at least equal to the resources of the poorer provinces under equalization.
- Traditional Native communities would be guaranteed a land base with adequate resources to feed, clothe and house our people.
- Indian control of Indian education would be a well accomplished fact.
- Unemployment in Indian and Native communities would, under these conditions, no longer continue at levels of 50% to 80% as they have through the past generation.
- Educated, working Indian and Native peoples would be building on the best of our own traditions through an informed use of modern technology.
- Peacemaker tribunals and other traditional ways of settling disputes within our own communities would have settled most complaints long before they would reach the courts.
- Traditional means of dispute resolution would also effectively prevent violence and abuse within the family.

Mr. Chairman, this could all sound like a utopian pipe dream if everything on this list had not been recommended on repeated occasions by parliamentary committees and public inquiries. We can not look seriously at the relationship between Native people and the justice system without being aware that all the conditions which foster and encourage conflict with the law have been sustained and perpetuated by government after government.

Who Benefits from the Present Condition?

When the time comes that there is a government in this country that is as willing to act on the words of the Native People as this inquiry is to hear us, two things will happen:

- *first*, the proportion of Native People in conflict with the law will be no more and perhaps less than the proportion of the general population; and,
- *second*, the need for prisons as we know them today will be called seriously into question.

Before we deal more specifically with the prison system, and ways to simply turn off the tap which keeps flowing our people into the prisons, there is a need to be aware of who is benefitting from the perpetuation of a political and economic setup, sanctioned under law, which keeps our people in a state of degradation.

Mahatma Gandhi wisely said, many years ago, that there is enough in this world for everyone's need but not enough for everyone's greed.

- How many of our people are forced to steal simply in order to live?
- How many of our young people fleeing to the city find that their best chance of making money is to sell their bodies?
- How do you justify the sentencing practices that sentences a young white man to jail for 90 days for rape while sending two Native women to the Prison for Women for seven and nine years for breaking school windows?

We do not need to name names to know who benefits from a society that gives legal sanction to these arrangements while failing to act on any number of reports that have the whole hearted endorsement of the leaders and elders of our communities. We need only be aware that

> *a people who are building empires are not concerned with building a humane family life. Empire builders must dispense with their humanity in order to serve the cause of the empire.*

The methods which are used against our people are more subtle and more complex today. Sadly, they are not less devastating.

Out of the Frying Pan: The Best Interests of the Children

Native and Indian communities in this country have faced the mass abduction of their children for the last four generations. For three generations we endured the residential schools. The horrors of those institutions have been documented to the point that I do not need to repeat those obscenities here.

In the 1960s, the residential schools were finally replaced. By what? By a system called the Children's Aid Societies. A peculiar mix of arrogance and ignorance that could decide that the deportation of our children from this province was "in the best interests of the children". Only a society founded on greed could have licensed, sponsored and funded the arrogance and ignorance of those Societies.

In my 12 years' experience of working in the prison system in this country, I have gotten to meet and talk with a great many Native inmates. If I have used strong language in talking about the treatment of our children, it is because there is nothing clearer in my mind than the conviction that what brought these people into prison was the anger and frustration at being cut off from the rightful inheritance of their communities. The abuse, neglect and ignorance which they endured in white foster homes — places considered to be "in the best interests" of our children — were, as often as not, breeding grounds for the hostile behaviour which led to their imprisonment.

I have known young men who were shipped as far away as Texas to face physical and sexual abuse when their parents could not provide a proper home for them but other near relatives could well and gladly have done so. By the time that I met this one young man he had a record of doing to others what his foster parents had done to him. The difference was two-fold: he was a Native person; and, he was caught and punished.

If I appear angry and bitter it is because I am here to represent the bitterness and the anger of our brothers and sisters with whom I have worked for the last dozen years in prisons across this country. I want to talk about alternatives to imprisonment. But I can not do that until I have made abundantly clear the root causes for the conflict which has been incarcerating our brothers and sisters.

A Society Without Prisons

When Champlain first sailed up the St. Lawrence River, there were no prisons in our societies. We did not need to imprison people. We did not have any prisons because we simply did not need them. We did not set up the levels of temptation. We did not create the levels of deprivation. And we did not abandon the fundamental laws of creation.

We did not try to own what can only belong to God.

We lived by a law that recognized our dependence on the land, and the water and the air. We did not think that we could own these things. We could only realize that we and the other creatures on the earth are the children of the Creator.

The Quakers take responsibility for the invention of the penitentiary. But the penitence they intended people to serve was not to exceed thirty days. In biblical times, a person might sell himself into slavery when he was destitute but he was to become free again after six years. And if he were beaten in any way that lost him so much as a tooth or a drop of blood he was to be let go.

The prisons which we have today are a product of modern civilization: a civilization whose national church is found in the shopping centre and the bank. The prisons are a form of sacrificial worship in which the Native people have become the burnt offering to whatever god it is that is worshipped in these places. This sacrificial prison system has also become a major industry. When we come to look at alternatives we need to be prepared to shut down that industry. The political masters of this society need to be prepared to kick the prison habit.

Our people also need to kick the prison habit. We have a pretty clear idea of what our alternatives will be. We know what a strong and healthy society looks like from the teachings of our elders and the traditions which we have received. We would like to hear from your elders and leaders what a strong and healthy society looks like to them; one that includes room and resources for our people.

Where Everyone is Related to Everyone Else

In a society where everyone is responsible for the well being of everyone else we did not need to lock our doors. In a community where everyone is related to everyone else and most of a person's business is conducted in public there is not much point in lying.

Our own ways did not leave a lot of room for anti-social behaviour for two reasons. First, because the ways in which each person was responsible for the well being of every other person and for the community as a whole were very clearly spelled out. This meant that there was neither need nor incentive for the kinds of misbehaviour that most frequently land our people in trouble today.

Secondly, because when we live in harmony with the cycles of the Creation there can not be the accumulation of wealth which creates vast differences between the different classes of society. The visitor society — the dominant culture in North America — is quickly reaching the point of choking on its own garbage, asphyxiating from man-made oxygen deprivation, and destroying itself by setting one class against another.

It would be tempting to say that such a society can not long endure. Unfortunately, we have seen imperial societies continue to endure and to heighten the oppression of their captive peoples for hundreds of years after they have past their prime. When I say that our people are the miner's canary, I can only hope that if the dominant culture indeed has elders and leaders they will take heed of the drooping canary in ways that they have not yet been prepared to do.

The Geneva Conventions and Canadian Prisons

Earlier this year I was called by the psychologist at a prison in which a young man was holding a hostage. Sadly, I was too far away to reach the prison in time to make much difference.

The inmate had been shot and killed. He was not shot in a way that would disable him and allow his hostage to be freed. He was shot in a way that could only have killed him.

What was the weapon of choice? The dum-dum expanding bullets that are prohibited by the Geneva Conventions on War are standard issue in our prisons. How do we come to use against inmates ammunition that is prohibited to use on a field of battle? When we see the disproportionate number of Native people in prisons does this not seem to be a license to do to Native people what the Conventions on War prohibit us from doing to enemies at war?

Family: The Place to Begin

We can only begin to address the problem of the numbers of Native people in prisons by having Native communities take responsibility for our own people at every possible level. This needs to happen in the cities as well as in reserve communities. The largest numbers of our people move back and forth between their home communities and the cities with some regularity.

Children

This province has made far greater strides than Ontario where I live, at least in the field of child welfare. In Ontario, we have a law on the books which would allow Native child welfare organizations to assume responsibility for our own children in the cities, and in Métis and non-status communities. We also have a Ministry who are intent on destroying the good intentions expressed in the legislation and a majority government that does not seem concerned to see the Native provisions in the *Child and Family Services Act* brought into reality.

But the place to begin to turn off the tap and stop our people from going into prisons can only be with the rebuilding of Native and Indian family life. We have to re-gain control of our community services of all kinds, including education.

Old People

We need housing and services for our old people in the communities. And when we develop those services, we will see that there is a very real role for our old people to fulfil in regard to children. I do not think there was ever a time when the nuclear family thrived without the support of an extended family.

Parents who are able to work outside the home need to look to grandparents, elder aunts and uncles and others for the care of their children. The elderly, in turn, need to have real and important things to do. Much as teen age children need real and important things to do.

Whether a reserve is another kind of prison, a bantustan or a real opportunity to develop our own self-government depends entirely on the degree of control we, as Native people, achieve over our own lives within our communities. Whether the city is simply a pitfall and a sink hole for our people or a genuine economic opportunity depends equally on the extent to which we are able to build our own community services within the city.

A Healing Place

We need to create healing centres in every Native and Indian community in this land. A healing centre is a place where people turn to their own brothers and sisters for the healing that they need. They also turn to their elders and spiritual teachers in the same place. A place where healing deep emotional wounds is part and parcel of the same process in which a person finds the best education for their children, job re-training for themselves, or various kinds of social assistance.

A Learning Centre

The child who comes into this world is a spirit being. His presence is a gift to the whole community. When the community can not accept that gift by caring for the child an immeasurable harm is inflicted on that spirit being. The community that is not able to accept the gift of a child is a sore and troubled community. The healing place that it needs must be the central focus of the community. The community that does not fulfil its responsibility for the well-being of every child is bound to have visited upon itself the abuse that it has heaped on its children.

A healing place needs to be the corner-stone of our own educational system as well as the foundation for replacing the parole system. For the youngest child, it provides an education founded on a series of healthy experiences in which the child learns to develop the skills to become a responsible member of the community.

The moral and ethical tools — the sense of responsibility — is more readily learned in a traditional setting. But the growing child who has learned to be a part of the community will need and want to learn the more advanced technical skills that make him a more effective member of the community.

Unfortunately, we will also need to give our children the coping skills they will need to deal effectively with a society in which lying is often a matter of presenting the best defense available. We need to teach our children not only the values of our own society but also help them to understand that there is a culture out there that stands for everything opposite to the ways of the Creation. At the same time, we need to help them understand that not everyone who looks different shares the attitudes of the dominant culture.

We need to educate our children to the ways of the Creator while training them to cope with the ways of the dominant culture. The conflict which lands so many Native children in trouble is inevitable unless they receive this special kind of bicultural education. Only those of our elders who have struggled to recover our own culture and also struggled to cope with the dominant culture can provide the preventive education our children need.

Rehabilitation

For every one of our brothers and sisters who are in prison there are another ten who are no less wounded but have simply, by the Grace of God, managed not to come into direct conflict with the law. We need to provide the opportunity for these people to develop in adolescence, mid-life or even in their later years the positive experience which was earlier denied to them.

Half Way House

The Native person goes into prison because he has acted out the wounds inflicted on him by this society. And he comes out of the prison more wounded than when he went in. The man or woman coming out of prison needs a double healing. They need the positive experience of a genuine community that everyone else needs. They also need to rid themselves of the bitterness of an experience that was never intended to serve any purpose of rehabilitation.

I was the founding chairman of the only Native half way house in Ontario. I named it for one of my dearest friends, Newbery House. When I see the control that the Correctional Service continues to exercise over the people coming into Newbery

House I am not sure that we have honoured my friend or favoured our brothers.

Nobody is going to learn to function in this society after being incarcerated for so many years without making a mistake. Yet the control over these people is no less severe than if they were still in prison. Indeed, the half way house is classified as an extension of the minimum security prison. On one occasion, when a parolee had made a mistake, but not one that hurt anyone but himself, we tried to intercede. We were told quite bluntly, *"We are gods. We can send anyone back to prison any time that we want."*

Far from being a healing centre, this half way house has degenerated into a perpetuation of the disease it was intended to cure.

We need to have a place where our wounded warriors, our displaced people can come to learn how to live again in harmony with the Creation. I do not think we would turn away a non-Native person in search of the same healing. But we can not wait until the powers that be and the majority of the dominant culture are ready for that healing.

Tearing Down the Walls

The dilemma that we face as Native people is that we can not wait for the visitor society to wake up to what is happening to its empire as it visibly collapses around us. We need to pull together our people and renew our knowledge of living together in harmony with the rest of Creation.

This is not an easy task when our young people see around them a life that seduces with the veneer of luxury overlaying the reality of personal, national and world debt.

The time for empire building has past. We can not rebuild the family without also being concerned to rebuild the environment which the forces of the empire have done so much to destroy.

Long before the visitor people came to our land we were warned by the prophecies of what lay ahead. We were told that a people would come who would need to tear us away from our relationship with the Creator. But we were also taught that this would serve the purpose of enabling us to renew our strength in our own ways. And that it would also serve the purpose of allowing the visitor people to learn to live like human beings are meant to live on this land.

We were also warned in the prophecies that there would be two different kinds of visitor peoples: those who came with a face of anger and those who came with a face of brotherhood. We see that those who came with a face of anger are the empire builders, the ones who mainly hold the economic and political power in the dominant culture. And those who come with the face of brotherhood are, beneath the skin, much like ourselves, and our doors remain open to them.

Changing Faces

Perhaps there are also those who are able to change their face. Perhaps there are those who will see that the devastation that has been done to the First Nations of this land is now happening to the land and all its people.

When the dominant culture becomes ready to stop destroying the land and the air and the water it will begin to understand what it was Big Bear meant when he said, "The time will come when my people will be of great service to this country."

When that time comes, I think Mr. Chairman, that what I am about to say about prisons will also be understood. And, if that time does not come soon, then this world will be destroyed by the hands of fools who are greedy enough to let their own brothers and sisters suffer rather than to share the gifts of the Creator.

A Blasphemy in the Face of God

When I look around at what I see inside the prisons, what I see is an unending variety of ways of degrading and damaging human beings. I see nothing very much that can seriously be called rehabilitation. I see nothing very much that will give to inmates a desire to live a different life than the one that got them in there in the first place. I do see a tremendous educational process that will mainly teach inmates how to do better the next time.

What prison teaches is "tit for tat", the karma of retribution. This is the central lesson of the dominant culture at large as our people experience it. The difference in prison is that the lesson is inflicted with much greater force on those who either did not learn well enough on the outside, or who learned everything all too well except how to avoid getting caught.

Who Controls the Prisons

I have met any number of wardens in this country and abroad. I have met wardens who are sincerely dedicated to improving the situation of Native inmates in terms of their opportunity to practise Native spirituality. No doubt these same basically good people want to increase the opportunity of every inmate to do something constructive with their lives.

But the warden who impressed me most was the one I met on the Island of Mauritius at a conference of the World Council of Churches after he had left the correctional system to become a Methodist minister. In the years since that trip, every observation I have made inside a prison confirms that gentleman's view that the prisons are controlled by the guards. The administration can be filled with all kinds of good intentions without ever penetrating the system controlled by the guards.

I am also in touch with a small corps of guards from different parts of the country who meet periodically to find ways to carry out their role in a more constructive way, particularly in regard to Native people. The dialogue with these guards is useful because it brings together a group of concerned human beings. And whatever kindness they might do while they continue in their job as guards is a blessing. But my own best guess is that those guards who are truly moved to a deeper understanding of humanity will not long remain in that job.

Alternatives to Prison

There is nothing so much in need of correction in Canada as the Correctional Service of Canada.

We will not succeed in correcting the penal system until we become prepared to lower the level of violence in the society at large. When we become prepared to lower the level of violence we will find that there is very little need to maintain the prison system at all.

The alternatives to prison have been documented time and time again by Native leaders and by scholars of every kind. There have been as many reports on reforming the prison system as there have been on improving the lot of Native peoples. The reports on the prison system have by and large received the same degree of rejection in actual practise as the ones on Native conditions.

Conclusion

This paper was written by a cherished friend of many years, a professional writer who is well versed in the ways of governments and bureaucracies by personal experience.

But it does not speak to my personal sense of outrage against the atrocities that were committed down through the centuries and are still being committed against us by the police and the courts and the prison system of Canada.

It does not speak to my sense of outrage against the Children's Aid Societies of Canada who have worked so diligently and deliberately to destroy Native families in their superior and arrogant belief that they knew best.

It does not speak to the reality that most of our people in the prisons started out by being ripped off from their families by Children's Aid and became lost people without roots as a result.

It does not speak to the unutterable lack of humanity and sense of common decency that exists within the parole boards of Canada.

It does not speak to the violence of police and courts and prison guards as that violence is continually and deliberately practised against us.

We are surrounded by racist hatred which is practised every day on the streets and wherever we go, racism is practised openly and covertly. Racism is alive and well in Canada and there is no justice for the aboriginal people of Canada in the courts of Canada.

The reality for the aboriginal people of Australia is precisely the same, except that the Churches of Australia are picking up their responsibility and expressing their outrage against a system which is out of control.

When Christopher Columbus landed in North America not one Native person was in prison because there were no prisons. We had law and order because law was written in the hearts and minds and souls of the people and when justice had to be applied it was tempered with mercy.

The laws came from the ceremonies which were given by the spirit people, the invisible ones. As a people we were less than perfect as all other people are, but we had no prisons because we didn't need them. We knew how to live and we also knew how not to live.

I do not propose to talk about alternatives to prison because a question so serious must be dealt with at another place and another time where we can assess the sincerity of those who propose alternatives. We have always had alternatives. But nobody would ever listen to us. Perhaps now is that time when some people are capable of listening.

THE PAROLE BOARD

The National Parole Board is simply another arm of the prison.
It is simply another face of the Beast.
It is a blasphemy in the face of God.
Its only purpose seems to be to keep the prisons full
and when people are let out on parole they are required
to live more perfectly than Jesus Christ did.
There is no mercy for anyone who makes even a minor mistake.
It's back to prison for anyone who does.
We operate a Native halfway house in Sudbury Ontario which is
funded by C.S.C. which means total control by C.S.C.
And the parole board members in Sudbury
make sure it stays that way.
As long as we dance to their drum we will continue to get
simply an extension of the prison system *without bars*.
We have alternatives that we could use but
we are not allowed, because total control
is the name of the game.
And there is no hope for improvement.
As long as it stays that way,
prisons are simply an extension of empire.
It is nothing more than an industry.
To say that it corrects anything is a lie,
because it simply multiplies the evil
at incalculable cost to everyone
especially the victims and their families.
Two wrongs can never make a right,
not even today.

Our people were told
long before the white man came to this sacred land,
that a people would come who would have white faces
but no eyes and ears.
They would also have two faces,
one would be the face of brotherhood,

everything would be good.
But if they came with a face of anger,
it would be very hard for us.
Well it's very obvious which face they came with.
It was also told that they would build places with stone walls
that we know as prisons today.
And it was said that the time would come
when the guns would melt in their hands
and those places that we call prisons would totally
disintegrate and the materials that they were built
would return to the earth as it was before.
And even the memory of them
would be wiped from the minds of the people.

THERE WILL BE JUSTICE

OPENING THE BIRD CAGES

What I am doing I see as
liberating the birds.

Opening the cage doors
and letting them fly where they want.

To help the people to do
what they need to do to assert themselves,
to do things of value to themselves.

I call it opening the bird cages.
That's what I call it.

Once the cages are open,
the birds can fly wherever they want.

The sky's the absolute limit.

ON THE ENVIRONMENT

To my Sisters and Brothers in this Forum on the Environment: I
have these words to say, but they may not be nice words to hear.

One of our Native holy men of long ago said.
"What is the life of a man?"
It is like the flash of a firefly in the night,
it is like the breath of a buffalo in the winter,
It is like the shadow that runs across the grass and disappears
into nowhere.

Those who destroy the earth will be destroyed
        by the power of the earth

because the Earth Mother has not lost her power
and the elements
the lightening and the thunder and the great winds,
the sun and the moon and the stars,
they have not lost their power.

This is a fool's paradise
where people lurch from one panic to another.

There is a price to pay
and the time is very near when it has to be paid
for the destruction of the environment,
and people living now will have to pay.
It is called the great purification.

There are many prophesies in the Indian world
that talk about what would happen to us
after those strange people came across the ocean
with their strange ways.

> *they came in violence,*
> *they have lived in violence,*
> *and they will go in violence.*

But it will not be the violence
of the Aboriginal people of this sacred Turtle Island.

It is not within our power to do that,
but in the hands of God
who will restore peace and tranquillity on the earth again.
Because there will be justice,
not only for people but for all living things on the earth.
After all these years, I finally understand
what was meant in the Bible where it says,
"the meek shall inherit the earth."
We have been dealing with criminal, captive, state governments
down through the years
whose policy has been and still is a policy of total genocide
against the Native nations of this sacred land,
it is a crime against humanity
it is evidenced in the Innu land of Labrador
and at Little Buffalo Lake in Alberta
and in other places like stealing the trees
from the people in British Columbia.
We have to stand virtually alone against *the Beast*
who never stops devouring.

Progress and development,
We have always been told
That we have to have progress and development.
But we know it by another name,
its called *death and destruction*,
to the earth and the people of the earth,
wherever *the man* has put his hand on the earth
and the people of the earth
there has come destruction and death to the people.
The man has to pay for those millions of deaths.
Because the people of the earth are part of the creation too.
Never in the history of the human family
has the Earth and the children of the Earth Mother
been so devastated as it is now.

We the Aboriginal people have never willingly or mindlessly
destroyed the creation around us
because we have always understood that it belongs only to the
one who created it
and to the ones who will come after us *(our grandchildren)*
and when we sat in council together
we had to consider the well being of those
who would come to live on this earth
for seven generations into the future.
In contrast to that is a society that devours everything
including their children's inheritance.
The insatiable greed for money and power is responsible for
that. Competition is a sacred word in the marketplace,
that word comes from that great evil negative power
who is determined to destroy God's creation.
But this world will not be destroyed by the hands of fools
neither by nuclear holocaust or by human destruction,
that is guaranteed.
The International Monetary Fund and the World Bank
through the transnational corporations and governments
are responsible for most of the destruction today
and greed for money and power are the root of it,
and we support those corporations and governments by the
colossal and mindless waste of the earth's resources,
we can't do that for much longer.
There is a prophesy in this land that says.
"One day the money will die." What then?
Will we know how to co-operate with each other?
Or will we still compete?

THE END OF THE EMPIRE

Dr. Gillian Baker of New York was asked to write
something for the United Nations 25 years ago.
She produced a 48 page booklet describing
9 previous empires before this one.
From the Sumerian Empire 8 thousand years before Christ,
she described each empire in text and graphs.
It appeared that each empire in turn walked
as though in lock step.
Down through the centuries,
each of them came to their highest point of arrogance
and disappeared from history.
She said of the United States of America
that their highest point of arrogance
was when they dropped those two bombs,
on Hiroshima and Nagasaki,
and surely,
there is no question about the declining empire of the U.S.A..
Dr. Gillian Baker said that the U.S.A. would collapse by 1982.
Well it hasn't obviously,
— *but it is a money empire.*
One of the old prophesies of the indigenous people of this land
spoke of the time *when the money will die.*
Looking at the world monetary situations of the past 20 years,
and the impossible debt load
that so many poor nations are saddled with
Says to me the money will die before the year 2000.
And money is the blood of the Beast.

March 20, 1990
Toronto, Ont.

HEALING COMMUNITIES

We have to create healing communities.
We have to do that or we die.
Our children will die.
They will destroy themselves and each other
if we keep going as we are going now.
We have to think seriously about where we are going.
We cannot do anything with *superficial thinking*.
We are in crisis, what will we do?
An how will we do it?
A wise man once said:
"The people will always know what to do"
provided they have the context in which to do it.
Man has always made sure that we have no context.
What to do?
He has the money.
He has the laws.
He has the prisons.
Are we helpers?
No, we are not helpers unless we choose to be.
We are an extremely intelligent and resourceful people.
We could never have made it for countless thousands of years,
in this sacred land,
if we didn't know how to take care of ourselves
and each other.
Now we must return back to that same resourcefulness again.
Our strength is in our togetherness.
Our weakness is in our aloneness.
As long as we don't care about each other and for each other
we will all be alone and we will be destroyed *one by one*.
That great evil one is using people and ideas and material
things to divide us.
He is determined to destroy God's creation
through destroying us
because we are a part of God's creation and we have a lot of

power within us;
the name of that power is love.
His weapons are lies, confusion, deception, etc.
Our only weapon is truth and the power of love.
Those are the only two weapons that we have
but they are invincible and they are given to us directly
by the creator God.

TWO-WAY LIBERATION

As a person liberates himself/herself,
she's also liberating her oppressor
from the trap that he's got in.

So it's a beautiful time ahead.

If we don't screw it up.

FAMILY HEALING

It is for me an imperative that we learn how to heal ourselves, our communities, and our Nations, because we are the final teachers in this sacred land.

What we have to teach the strangers who came to this land is how to live in harmony with the creation which means, first, for men and women to live in harmony together. We cannot teach that unless we first know how to do it for ourselves. I am speaking of Native or Aboriginal people because that is my greatest concern. It has been my concern for the past 35 years. Violence against women, violence against children . . . there is a cause, it doesn't happen by itself, there is a reason for violence against women. We as people can't get any lower. We have to learn how to heal ourselves and healing ourselves is the hardest part. When we learn how to heal ourselves the rest will be easy, you just watch and see it happen. If we are still the good people that we once were it will happen very fast. We cannot live the way we are, in total disharmony, because we will not survive the purification that is coming towards us very fast.

There is an old Cheyenne proverb that says, when our women's hearts are on the ground it's finished. No matter how strong our warriors are or how good their weapons, it's finished. There's nothing left to live for.

Our women have a sacred work to do in this part of creation. They take from man and they take from God and they return those gifts in the most beautiful way in the form of new human beings, new spirit beings. What other way do we have? We have no other way because our women carry the doorway to life for all humanity.

We need our women and our women need us. Edna Manitowabi says that our women are created complete but our men are not. Does that answer the question of why a man always has to return to his woman to find the ecstasy of his completeness? For me the creator God is both totally male, and totally female. It is within that totality, that completeness, that ecstasy, that God is. We have been taught that God is male only. We have had a patriarchy for over 2000 years which has been very hurtful to our women as well as to our men and to our children. It has been a distortion of the reality. We as created human beings are both male and female. We have both qualities within us but one predominates. Men can be nurturing and affirming as well as women can. Men have by and large lost that quality of nurturing and affirmation by the violence of the world that they have to live in, and the images that they are constantly presented with. If we want to heal as men and women we have to bring back the image of the Goddess again. We have to bring the image of the Goddess back into our hearts and our minds, and our souls. The Goddess represents gentleness, affirmation, life. She also represents woman/eternal woman.

I say that women are the foundation of our Nations. Some say that they are the backbone of our Nations. This is why I have had to help women for the past thirty five years to help restore them to their rightful place again in the human family. A helper is all that I can be. What we need as Native Nations more than anything else is strong clear minded women. Strong clear minded women automatically make strong clear minded men. Women have to ask the creator and each other "what did the creator have in mind when she created women?" Men have to ask the same question of the creator too.

The first man and the first woman created lived in total harmony. They had no choice. They had no need to be or to live otherwise. But look at us now, there's hardly a man and a woman who can live in peace and harmony. Why?

Well for one thing we have all come through compulsory miseducation and the politics of education. We have lost sight of why we are and our purpose in life. The prophets said that these strangers who came would have no eyes and no ears. Those are the ones who taught us the new way and it was miseducation. They created an artificial reality. They said "it's a 'dog eat dog' world out there and if you want to survive you have to be like us".

The residential schools did a tremendous amount of harm to us. They ripped apart our families. We are still living with that legacy whether we realize it or not. The succeeding governments and the society around did everything in their power to make us disappear. Why? Because we were *not like them*! They have hated our guts. They have despised us. They have done everything in their power to make us disappear; but we are still here and we will remain here because we belong to the land. The land belongs to God, it does not belong to us. We can only be the care-takers for the generations to come after us. We have the responsibility to keep it clean and beautiful for them. We also have the responsibility to learn again how to be the beautiful people that we once were.

The man's way has always been an obsession with power, with having things, with possession, with personal prestige, with fame and glory, with power over others especially power over women. And this way was never our way. We once had power *with* women which was the only right way to be. Now things are in a mess until we get back to the right way again.

We have healing circles for women. We have healing circles for men. But, will we ever have healing circles for men and women together? I propose that is the next step for us to take. If we can do it with just a few people to make a beginning, we can surely do it with a larger crowd as time goes on. We have been divided into two solitudes for much too long. Women and men have lived separately. We have drifted apart each in our separate ways. It was never like that long ago. Women had an equal voice with men. We always listened to the wisdom of women. We can not put it together separately and have it right.

It was not God who messed-up the world the way it is now. It was human beings, and it is human beings who have to fix it right again . . . That means us.

We have bought into that way, the wrong teaching that was brought here by those strange people from across the ocean. We have the medicine to change the way things are. It is called L.O.V.E. We all have our share. It is replenished every day. The more we give away the more we are given in return. This teaching is given in the 10 commandments. That is how we lived for thousands of years before we ever heard of it. We didn't talk about it, we lived it every day of our lives. If we could do it then, we can learn how to do it again.

What we have to do is to take hold of the present and make the future what we want it to be. We have the power to do that. We do not need guns or violence. If we want to change the world and make it a more beautiful place to be, the only place to begin is in our own hearts and minds.

To create a healing circle is simple and easy. All we need is a few people who want to sit down and together to try to find their healing by sharing their pain, their confusion, their hurts, their lack of understanding etc, etc.

Last year in Montreal I was asked to do a healing circle for men. There two women who came into my workshop, I welcomed them. One woman spoke very well about her own pain. The other woman spoke eloquently of another family where she had witnessed brutality over a long period of time. It was a real blessing to have those two women in the workshop because women can articulate so well. But . . . men need more time, there were twelve or fifteen men in that workshop, they spoke very little. The men needed to experience a healing workshop a few times to get comfortable with it. Another point that is vitally important to men is that a man has to present an image of strength; certainty not only to his woman and his family, but to every one else he encounters. For that reason it is extremely hard for a man to expose himself in an emotional way whereas it is more natural for a woman. We need healing circles for women and men together. We need to be sharing together again.

November 10, 1992

A WOMAN IN REPOSE

From out of those eyes
Looked the soul of a woman
She spoke silently
But eloquently
Of the mystery of woman
I knew that she was a child of God
And she is a part of that mystery
She spoke to my soul
Because that's the kind of communication that it was
She spoke of the beauty and the sacredness of woman
She looked no where in particular
But sat in repose
And her look spoke volumes to my soul
Because I looked back
And I saw the pain of woman
Down through the centuries
Till now

Our Women People and the Creation

Grandfather great spirit
We ask a blessing for our women people
that they may come to understand again
the sacred work that you gave to them
in the work of your continuing creation.   Meegwetch.

From the time that the invaders came to this land and set themselves to steal our rightful inheritance that was given us by the creator, our women have been degraded and debased and dishonoured, and we have watched for a long time with a great agony to see how low down our women have been degraded.

This is the way that I see our women. They were given very special gifts by the Great Spirit, the Creator. Those gifts are physical, mental, and spiritual. It was to the women people that he gave the special gift to bring the newborn children into the world and to take care of them so that our nations would be strong, and it was to our grandmother moon that he gave the work to regulate when the children would be born and it is also that our grandmother moon was given the work to regulate when the animal and the bird life and the fish life was to be renewed, each one in their season and it is our grandmother moon also that has the work to raise the great salt water night and day all over the earth and many other kinds of work she does with our mother earth that we no longer understand.

It is through our women that those who are still coming towards us, the unborn, will come, because that is the way that the great mystery made it to be and in no other way can it come about.

Our women are very closely related to our Mother Earth and that is why in some of the sacred dances of our people, the women had special dances in which they did not lift their feet off the earth. And like our Mother Earth, it is from our Mother's bodies that our first food comes to keep us growing until we are able to eat stronger foods. And it is our mothers who give us love and care and strength until we are able to stand alone and choose our own path in life.

There are many things that our women do for us, but we seem to forget that we should give honour to them, because we have learned that great negative way from the negative society around us.

It is our mothers who are our first teachers. They are the first ones to teach us our language and the true ways of our people. It is they who are the first ones to keep our nation strong and pure. They are the ones who teach us what love means because the great mystery who is the essence of love has put something of himself into each of then so that they would know by instinct how they should behave.

My understanding goes still further, because I believe this way about our women. I believe that just as they are the heart of our families they are also the heart of our nations, Ojibwa, Cree, Mohawk, or whatever nation, they are our source of spiritual power, they are our inspiration, they are our backbone, they are *the* heartbeat of our nations and we must have a strong and true heartbeat to be a strong people. If our heartbeat is weak, we will be weak. Those are some of the reasons why we must give honour to our women people like it was long ago.

And we must come to understand the lying ways that were used to discredit and dishonour our women and why that was done from the beginning. Because it was in that way that our most precious possessions, our women and our spiritual ways were debased and put down, and the more devastation that was done in that way the more devastated and demoralized we became as a people. So if we are going to stand as strong nations of Indian people again in this land that was given to our ancestors long ago, then we must return to that true way, what is called The Good Red Road; we must begin to respect our women and speak and act in an honourable way towards them, and in that way give honour to the great power who made them. But it is also that our women must come to understand the true ways that the creator made for them to walk on this earth, and in that way give honour to us their men people and honour to the creator who made us.

When we have learned to walk in that way again all things will become sacred and we will not have to wonder what tomorrow will bring.

It is a sad fact of life for us that the strangers who came to this land imposed a great oppression on us, they killed and they destroyed, they massacred our people, until like the sacred buffalo they had almost wiped out our ancestors, and it is recorded that because of their violent ways they actually obliterated some tribes of Native people in America, and it is also recorded that in what is now called California they hunted down and shot Indian people on sight, *for sport*. That oppression that began when the strangers came has not stopped for a minute, only the form is changed. But it is still as deadly as ever. It's called genocide, that is what the Canadian and the American governments are practising today on the Native people of North America; and they have proved many times over that they will not stop until we disappear as a people or become *like them*.

It is because of that oppression that we are obliged to become a warrior people and we must fight for the right to retain our humanity and our spirituality, and in that war our women stand shoulder to shoulder with us. They are warriors the same as we are, they are our strength and our inspiration.

Just as we get our strength and our medicines and our life from our earth mother we also get our strength and our sense of well being from the love of our women. It is they who make life worth living and freedom worth fighting and dying for, so we must support them and help them to become strong in the true ways again.

IN CONCLUSION

*All we are asking for from the people of Canada
is justice as Native People.*

There never has been any.

We have withstood the onslaught of Christianity and civilization, and we're still here. Many people are going to be celebrating the arrival of Christopher Colombus, this year.

We're going to celebrate the survival of us as nations. We are not tribes. We are Nations of Peoples. We have been put down for a long time. Five hundred years we have waited patiently for justice — to be accepted as children of the Creator. That's all we ask. We have that right.

We are not going to ask for justice from your criminal captive state governments, or from your criminal just-us system because there is none there.

But we're asking from the people of Canada for justice. *And we will have it.*

It's been a long wait. We have waited patiently, and we still honour and respect people of all colours of skin.

There are many stories; there are many prophecies in the Indian Land that talk about these stories. There is the prophecy of the seventh fire that talks about the time when "a people would come with hair the colour of fire" — red hair. The Norsemen came. — "But they wouldn't stay very long."

"And then there would be another people come after them with white skin, and wings" (sails) "on their canoes".

"But they would come with two faces. One was the face of brotherhood. And one was the face of anger."

We know what face they came with because we have lived with the longest holocaust of any people in the human family: the desecration of the earth and the people of the earth.

It's been a long hard story. But we're not complaining about the past. We're going to identify it. We're going to take hold of the present and make the future what we want it to be, because we are the final teachers in this sacred land. And all we have to do is teach our sisters and brothers how to live in harmony together as men and women.

We live in a total disharmony today. One of the things that we have to do if we want to heal as a people is to bring back the goddess to live within us, in our hearts and minds and in our souls — if we want to heal.

And it's a sick world — a terribly sick world. And as Mother Teresa said: "All it needs is love."

That's the one component that we never use.

Well, I guess that's all I'm going to say. Thank you for being here. Meegwetch!

Concordia University Convocation, Montreal, June 3, 1992.

A POSTSCRIPT FROM ART SOLOMON
AFTER A CONVERSATION WITH ONE OF HIS DAUGHTERS

It's been a pleasure to be here, you know.

Because a little bit more of the message
comes out.

I call myself a messenger.

*If you thought this was the last time you had
to give a message, what would you say?*

I'd say to hell with it.

I understood, you know,
for a number of years
that my responsibility in this world
is to do the best that I possibly can do
and to leave nothing undone that I can do
and leave the rest to the Creator.

So I can say to hell with it.

I've done what I could do today
and that's all.

PRINTED BY THE WORKERS OF
IMPRIMERIE D'ÉDITION MARQUIS
IN NOVEMBER 1994
MONTMAGNY (QUÉBEC)